A
Century
of
Scouting

Published by Boston Minuteman Council, Boy Scouts of America

Troop 11, Quincy, 1925.

Cover Illustrations:

<u>Front Cover:</u> **Scout Rally, Harvard Stadium, Circa 1917**. Thousands of Scouts attended this rally to demonstrate Scout skills. Flags from many towns including Newton and Wakefield are visible. (Courtesy: Private Collection)

<u>Back Cover:</u> (Left)
Camp Massasoit, Quincy Scouts, 1925. Camp inspection.
Troop 7, West Newton, 1923. Scouts in front of tent at "camp-out."
Scout Rally, Semaphore Demonstration, Circa 1917. Scouts learned and demonstrated semaphore (a method of signalling with flags) at rallies. Semaphore was commonly used by the military and railroads as a method of communicating over distance in a time before telephones and radio.

A
Century
of
Scouting

100 Years of Boy Scouts in Boston Minuteman Council, Boy Scouts of America

Editor: Fred O'Connell

Editorial Assistant: Madalina Bujorianu

Quincy Color Guard, 1925.

**Copyright © 2009 by
Boston Minuteman Council
Boy Scouts of America**

All rights reserved.

Boston Minuteman Council, Boy Scouts of America

Visit our website at www.BSABoston.org
where you can learn more about Boy Scouts in Boston
Go to www.MyScoutNews.org
to purchase additional copies of this book.

Printed in the United States of America

First Printing: November 2009

ISBN-978-0-615-33955-9

Cover design, copy, and book design by
Patricia Browne
Browne & Company
www.BrowneCompany.com

Contents

Camp Massasoit, Advertisement, 1944.
Notice that theme weeks were popular even in the 1940's.

"I was a boy once..."

Thus began Lord Robert Baden-Powell's Scouting for Boys, the book that contained the inspiration, the foundation, and the magic that grew into what we know today as the Boy Scouts. Over 100 years ago troops began to organize in the Boston area. They started in towns such as Dorchester, Quincy, Charlestown, Cambridge, and Lexington.

It started with a book and a few enthusiastic youth and adults who desired to be "Scouts".

Within these pages you will find the images of some of the tens of thousands of young men and women who have been part of the magical first hundred years.

Our hope is that it will inspire you to grow some of your own magic for the youth we serve today, so that their pictures and stories will make up the future editions for the next 100 years.

We want to thank all of those past and present volunteers who give so much of themselves to make a difference in the lives of young people in our Council. Special thanks to Fred O'Connell for making this book happen with a little help from his friends.

John R. Halsey
Council President

Matthew K. Thornton
Scout Executive

A Century of Scouting
History, Sources, and Bibliography

Putting together a book like this is a labor of love, and requires a certain stubborn belief that saving our history is a worthwhile endeavor. Peter Serette, of Boston Minuteman Council first proposed a book in 2003. A committee was formed but the book never moved past the idea stage. Committee member Fred O'Connell did not let go of the idea. He scoured bottom drawers, boxed up memories, and waited for the book project to be revived. When it was proposed to do a book to commemorate the first hundred years of Scouting in Boston, the Council put out a call for photos. We heard anecdotes about other people with great images and stories. But when it came time to get this book published, Fred was there with all his carefully preserved binders of photos.

Fred spent the summer of 2009 (and into the fall) selecting images, getting permissions to publish, gathering information for captions, and more. Intern Madalina Bujorianu organized information and created a database. It is because of their dogged determination that this book exists.

We hope that this book is just the first of many books that will capture our history. There were many people who contributed to this book. We have tried to list everyone, but if we missed someone's name, we apologize.

We would like to acknowledge the sources who contributed information or facts for this book:

Boston Minuteman Council Archives:
Unless otherwise attributed, all photos and memorabilia in this book are taken from the Boston Minuteman Council archives.

Camp Massasoit archives: A treasure-trove of old scrapbooks, clippings, camp memorabilia was found. We are in process of cataloging items. Items from the dining hall were also used as source material or illustrations.

T.L. Storer Scout Reservation archives: camp staff and troop photos taken over several decades were found in the camp office. Other things turned up in surprising places: Webelos slides in the eaves of the office, camp memorabilia in forgotten cabinets. We are in process of cataloging items.

Egan Center archives: Over the years, a file cabinet served as an informal repository of images and items. Most of our images from 1980-2000 came from this resource.

Special thanks to:

- **Troop 3, Somerville:** Early Scouting photos, old charters, and Scout memorabilia, especially some of our earliest images
- **Aaron Schmidt, Boston Public Library:** Print Department, Boston, Massachusetts
- **Jeff Barraclough, Lee Scouting Museum:** Manchester, New Hampshire. Large collection of Boston Minuteman Council items donated by a former Scouter who was active in that Council
- **Manny Bogaco, Howie Nelles:** Loon Pond information and photos
- **Andover Historical Society:** Andover, Massachusetts
- **Robbins Library:** Arlington, Massachusetts
- **Elizabeth Aykroyd:** Antrim, New Hampshire
- **John Munson:** Beacon Photography, Photographer for the King of Sweden event
- **Bruce Showstack:** Photography for various Scouting events including the King of Sweden breakfast.
- **Boy Scouts of America:** Irving, TX, Heidi Steppe, Legal Department
- **Boys' Life magazine**: Boy Scouts of America, Adryn Shackleford
- **L.A. Jones:** Milford, NH
- **Bob Wanamaker:** Milton, MA for photos, facts, and proofreading

Library Archives:

Antrim Public Library, Antrim, New Hampshire
Belmont Public Library, Belmont, Massachusetts
Cambridge Public Library, Cambridge, Massachusetts
Carey Memorial Library, Lexington, Massachusetts
Concord Public Library, Concord, Massachusetts
Lincoln Public Library, Lincoln, Massachusetts
Malden Public Library, Malden, Massachusetts
Medford Public Library, Medford, Massachusetts
Melrose Public Library, Melrose, Massachusetts
Milton Public Library, Milton, Massachusetts
Needham Public Library, Needham, Massachusetts
Reading Public Library, Reading, Massachusetts
Somerville Public Library, Somerville, Massachusetts
Thomas Crane Library, Quincy, Massachusetts
Wakefield Public Library, Wakefield, Massachusetts
Watertown Public Library, Watertown, Massachusetts
Winchester Public Library, Winchester, Massachusetts
Woburn Public Library, Woburn, Massachusetts

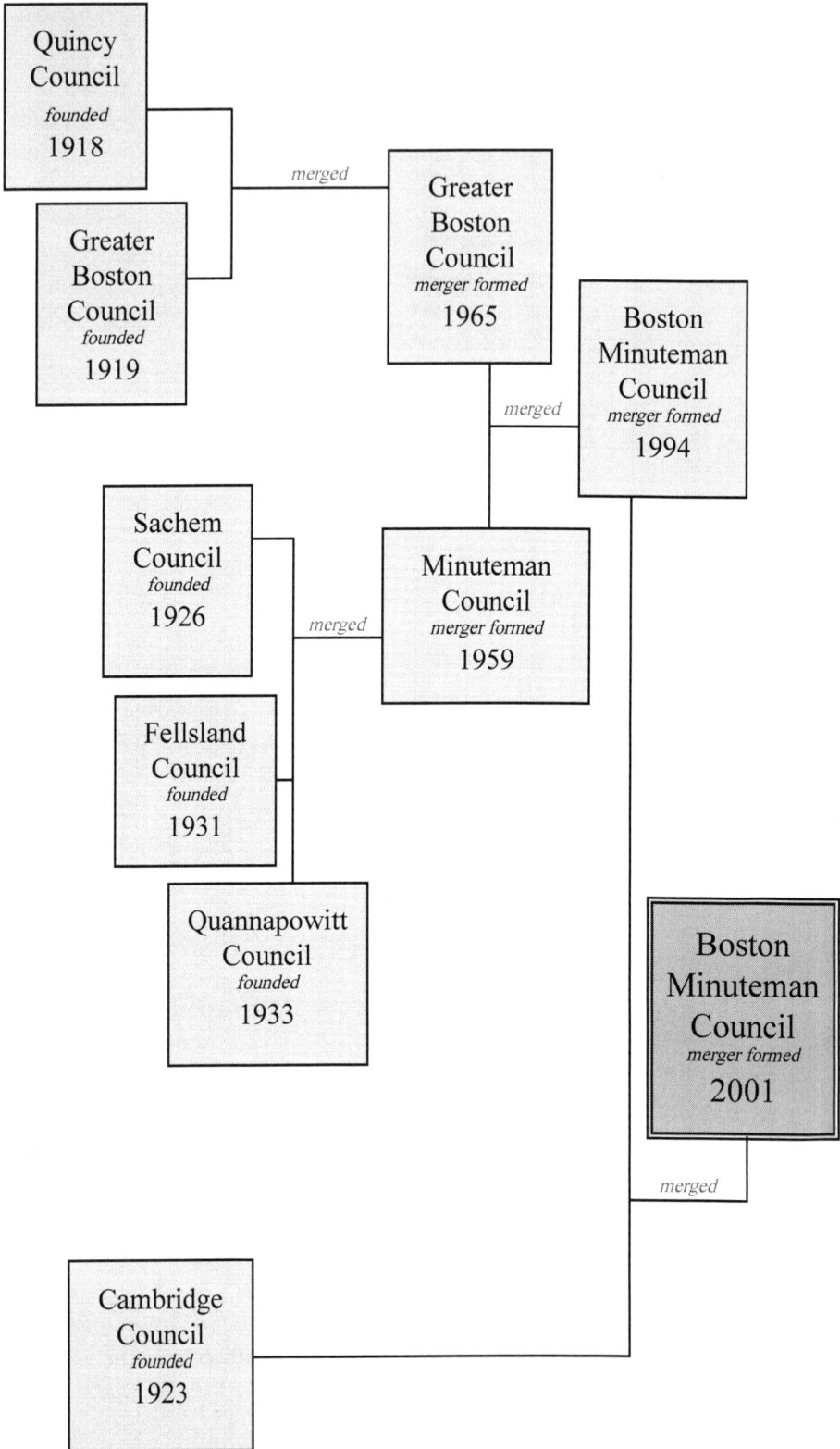

Quincy
Council
founded
1918

Greater
Boston
Council
founded
1919

merged

Greater
Boston
Council
merger formed
1965

Boston
Minuteman
Council
merger formed
1994

merged

Sachem
Council
founded
1926

merged

Minuteman
Council
merger formed
1959

Fellsland
Council
founded
1931

Quannapowitt
Council
founded
1933

Boston
Minuteman
Council
merger formed
2001

merged

Cambridge
Council
founded
1923

War to Peace:
Scouting's Unlikely Start

A childless, middle-aged, career-army man was an unlikely leader for one of the largest youth organizations in the world. But sometimes that is how stories begin...

British Army officer Colonel Robert Baden-Powell had already spent years in Africa and India when he was sent to South Africa in 1899. He quickly realized that his 500 British soldiers were wildly outnumbered by the Dutch colonial Boers, so he began making preparations to hold the strategic town of Mafeking for the battle he saw coming. He laid in supplies and prepared his men.

Baden-Powell
Circa 1900

When the Second Boer War began just months later, Baden-Powell's 500 soldiers were garrisoned in Mafeking, facing nearly 8000 Boers. With limited supplies and no hope of immediate relief from Britain, Baden-Powell used the one thing he had in abundance: his wits.

He engaged in a series of tricks to make the enemy think he was better prepared than he actually was. Baden-Powell ordered his men to bury fake land mines under full view of the enemy. His men pretended to avoid non-existent barbed-wire on the perimeter. He created fake spotlights out of cookie tins and lamps. He had one last secret weapon - a bunch of 12-15 year old boys he called the Mafeking Cadet Corps. They wore khaki uniforms and flat-brimmed hats while carrying messages, relieving guards, and working in the hospital, freeing up the troops to perform more critical duties.

Just before the siege began, Baden-Powell authorized publishing his military field manual for wilderness survival called Aids to Scouting for NCO's & Men. British relief troops arrived May 17, 1900, 217 days after the siege began. Baden-Powell was an instant celebrity. His Army manual became a must-read for boys all over the world.

Around 1900, there were several competing scouting groups. Ernest Thompson Seton wrote The Birch Bark Roll of the Woodcraft Indians and started the Woodcraft Indians in the United States. Woodcraft Indians drew on Seton's experience with nature, blended with Native American lore. Baden-Powell had a long fascination with Native American and African cultures. (Zulu wooden beads were the basis for the beads awarded in Wood Badge adult leader training.) In 1906, Seton and Baden-Powell met and shared ideas.

In 1908, eight years after the publication of Aids to Scouting, Baden-Powell published Scouting for Boys. He took a group of 22 boys camping to Brownsea Island, widely considered the first meeting of the Boy Scouts. Troops began to spontaneously form all over the world. Lieutenant-General Baden-Powell retired from the army in 1910 with the encouragement of King Edward VII who wanted him to concentrate on expanding Boy Scouts.

When Scouting officially arrived in the United States in 1910, there were several competing organizations. Ernest Thompson Seton's Woodcraft Indians, Dan Beard's Sons of Daniel Boone, and James West's Boys Brigade. Ultimately, from all these groups, Boy Scouts of America emerged.

Baden-Powell continued working and traveling to expand Scouting. In January 1912 when he was 55, he met 23-year old Olave St. Clair Soames who shared his birthday. They married in secret in October to avoid press coverage. Olave Baden-Powell was as committed to the Scouting Movement as her husband and sister-in-law Agnes (who started Girl Guides). Olave and Agnes encouraged family friend Juliette Gordon Low to bring Girl Scouts to America.

Baden-Powell continued to work for Scouting until 1937. He retired to Kenya where he died in 1941. His grave is marked with the "going home" trail symbol.

Going Home

Oh, and the father of Boy Scouts ultimately became a father himself. He and Olave had three children - one son and two daughters.

In 1910, there were three competing Scouting organizations in the Boston area: American Boy Scouts (ABS), New England Boy Scouts, and Boy Scouts of America (BSA). ABS was founded by publisher William Randolph Hearst. When Hearst resigned from ABS in December 1910 over fund-raising disputes, a New England-based ABS group formed calling itself New England Boy Scouts. In 1912, an ABS Scout shot another Scout at an ABS event. ABS never recovered from the bad publicity. By 1913, ABS and New England Boy Scouts had all but disappeared.

BSA continued to add members through the early 1910's. New troops were organized in nearly every town around Boston. Councils were formed in Quincy (1918) and Boston (1919). Scouting was seen as a positive activity by parents, and an adventure by the boys who eagerly joined newly formed troops.

First Scout Troop in Needham, 1911. These Scouts were marching in a Civic and Trade parade on the 200th Anniversary of the Town of Needham on September 19, 1911. Front, Donald Grant, Francis Powers, Donald Gray, Edward Croscup, Robert Morris. Back: Donald Hamilton, Lloyd Fleweiling, Robert Grant, Holly Cook and unknown. Scoutmaster Rev. John Waldon rode on the float.

Troop 13, Boston, Circa 1915. Scouting was only a few years old when this photo was taken. While it is unclear which town can claim the honor of having the first official Boy Scout troop in Boston Minuteman Council, Scouting was an immediate hit when Scouting reached America in 1910. Troop pride was evident in these smartly turned out Scouts with their Troop flag. In the ad below, the uniforms are described as "made of firm, strong khaki in a regular scout suit color... [consisting] of coat, trousers, leggings, and a hat." (Courtesy: Private Collection)

Newspaper Advertisement, Circa 1915. From the beginning, Scouts were encouraged to be enterprising and self-sufficient. Scouts who sold 24 bars of Olive Oil Castile soap could earn the $2.40 needed for a complete uniform.

Boy's Scout Suits

FREE

We are giving away Free these handsome, durable Boy's Scout Suits, just like the picture. They are made of firm, strong khaki, of regular scout suit color, and are trimmed with bright red braid. The suit consists of coat, trousers, leggings and hat, all in regular scout cut. Coat has brass buttons and red braid up and down front and on sleeves, pocket and collar. Full-length trousers have red stripe at side. Leggings lace up, have metal eyelet holes. Hat has wide stitched brim, and is true scout shape. We give Boy's Scout Suit complete, coat, trousers, leggings and hat, all together, for selling only 24 cakes of Olive Oil Castile Soap at 10c a cake. Write for Soap today. We send it express prepaid. When sold return $2 40, and we send this full Scout Suit, just exactly as described above **FRIEND SOAP CO.,**
1 Washington St., Dept. 931, Boston, Mass.

14

SCOUTMASTER'S GUIDE

SECOND DISTRICT
(DORCHESTER, ROXBURY and SO. BOSTON)
GREATER BOSTON COUNCIL
BOY SCOUTS OF AMERICA
1918

SCOUTMASTER'S GUIDE

For the Second District of the Greater Boston Council, Boy Scouts of America.

Dorchester, Roxbury and South Boston.

October, 1918.

Compiled from practical experiences and from such textbooks as the Handbook for Boys. First Aid for Boys, The Boy Scout Movement applied by the Church, Scoutmasters' Handbook, and the Rules and Regulations of the Greater Boston Council.

Material selected and arranged by

GEORGE W. FRENCH, District Executive

and

CLAYTON H. ERNST, District Commissioner.

Scoutmaster's Guide, 1918. Boy Scouting was still a relatively new organization, and local councils created their own guides to help Scoutmasters successfully organize and run their Troops. This is the cover and inside front page of the guide written for Dorchester, Roxbury, and South Boston Scoutmasters.

Scoutmaster Certificate, 1910. Edward Henry Kissler was appointed as Scoutmaster to the First Troop, City of Boston. According to the 1910 US Census data, Mr. Kissler was 25 years old and living on Mount Vernon Place, Beacon Hill. His occupation is described as "social work."

No. 229

Boy Scouts of America

HEADQUARTERS
124 East 28th Street
New York City

This Certifies that   Edward Henry Kissler

has received the approval of the National Council of the Boy Scouts of America, and is hereby duly appointed SCOUT MASTER of First Troop of the City of Boston

State of   Massachusetts

In Witness Thereof, the Seal of the Boy Scouts of America is herewith attached this   Twentieth   day of   August   1910

John L Alexander
Managing Secretary

15

BOY SCOUT COUNCIL IS FORMED HERE

At Meeting Held in High School Last Evening

At a meeting of gentlemen interested in the movement in the reception room of the High school building last evening a Boy Scout Local Council was formed. Among the gentlemen present at the meeting were Ex-Mayor G Louis Richards, Charles H Wesley, Representative Truman H Hawley, Frank E Poland, principal of the Daniels school, J Lewis Wightman, principal of the Faulkner school, Charles A Snell, principal of the Maplewood school, George H Johnson, member of the school board, C W Bradley Jr, L W Smith, Dr Frank W Plummer, Irving L Decatur, Arthur Plummer and Dr Corey H Chester.

The meeting was called to order by Representative Hawley. Dr Chester was elected temporary chairman and Lincoln W Smith temporary secretary. The purpose of the meeting was explained by Mr Bradley.

The election of officers resulted as follows:

First vice president—Arthur L Lee
Second vice president—Mr Ernst
Third vice president—S K Nason
Secretary—Hugh L Walker
Treasurer—W T Smallman
Scout commissioner—C W Bradley Jr.

Boy Scout Council in Malden, 1912. During the early days of Scouting, organization of Scouts was open to interpretation. What we know as Troops were also called Patrols or Councils. What is evident, though, is that local communities were excited and enthusiastic about Scouting.

SCOUTS HELP DELIVER COAL

Boy Scouts are Helping Women by Carrying Boxes of Coal to their Homes

"A Scout is helpful." Boy Scouts of Quincy are carrying out this one of their scout laws by helping many of the unfortunate women and children who have been forced to transport bags and boxes of coal to their homes. It is a common sight to see a poor old lady feebly pushing a baby carriage load of coal or to see a little child pulling a sled load of this precious fuel until they nearly drop with over-exhaustion. Patrols of Quincy's Boy Scouts are stationed at each coal yard and when some unfortunate is attempting to carry a heavy load, the scout runs up with a cheerful smile and gives the struggler a real lift. This is a scout's "good turn" and he never takes a "tip."

ORGANIZATION IS PERFECTED

Local Council of Boy Scouts Organized with S. T. MacQuarrie as President

Newspaper Articles, Quincy Council, Circa 1918. There were frequent stories about Scouts in local papers. The story about the coal (left) talked about the "good turn" the Scouts performed by assisting women hauling home coal for heating and cooking while many husbands and sons were off fighting during WWI. Other articles talked about the growth of Scouting and reported news about camps, rallies, and Scouting events. All this publicity raised the profile of local Scouting - making the Quincy Council a vibrant, fast-growing organization.

Troop 1, Quincy, 1911. This group photo was taken just months after Boy Scouts officially came to the United States. Note the uniforms: jackets, pants, leather leggings, and flat-brimmed hats, much like the uniforms described for the Mafeking Cadet Corps.

Robert Baden-Powell, Boston Visit, 1912. On February 1, 1912, Lieutenant General Robert Baden-Powell, founder of Boy Scouts, visited Boston in the company of James E. West, chief of Scouting in the United States. They met with 2000 Scouts from all over New England. Baden-Powell reviewed Scout drills at Boston Latin school. He met Governor Foss and Mayor "Honey Fitz" Fitzgerald. Baden-Powell spent time speaking about the true aim of Scouting: not to create soldiers, but rather to promote good citizens through individual character, "handy craftsman," and public service. Baden-Powell reported that there were already 400,000 Scouts in America - less than 2 years after Scouting was officially established in the United States.

GENERAL BADEN-POWELL ARRIVES IN BOSTON

BOY SCOUT LEADER REVIEWS NEW ENGLAND LADS AT LATIN SCHOOL —TO BE THE GUEST OF THE CITY CLUB

Lieutenant General Sir Robert S. S. Baden-Powell, K. C. B., K. C. V. O., hero of the Mafeking siege in the Boer War and founder of the British Boy Scouts, is the guest here today of 2000 Boy Scouts from all parts of New England. He arrived at the South Station from New York at 7 A.M. and will return on the midnight train, in company with James E. West, national chief scout executive of the Boy Scouts of America.

While here General Baden-Powell is being entertained at the Boston City Club. This afternoon he reviewed the visiting Scouts in the drill hall at the Boston Latin School. This evening he will be the guest of honor at a full dress military banquet at the Boston City Club, after which he will be escorted to Tremont Temple, where he will deliver an illustrated lecture on "Scouting In Peace and War."

BOY SCOUTS ARE CAMPING IN THE BLUE HILLS RESERVATION.

Scouts Camp in Blue Hills, 1912. This <u>Boston Globe</u> feature story describes a reporter stepping off a trolley car into the "wilds of the Blue Hills," met by two Scouts who escorted him to the camp. This camp was probably near the site of the present AMC camp on Ponkapoag Pond. Boston Minuteman Council headquarters are currently located in the Blue Hills, just about a mile from where these Scouts camped.

Scouts to Have Camp, Quincy, 1919. During the early years of Scouting, more than a dozen camps in the Boston area were purchased or donated, allowing local Scouts to have a accessible outdoor experience. This article talks about the formation of Camp Merrymount on Oldham Pond in Pembroke, MA. Cost for a week of camp? $6 per Scout.

SCOUTS TO HAVE A SUMMER CAMP

Qnincy Boy Scouts Are to Have Summer Camp on Oldham Pond Pembroke

FINDS SUMMER CAMP-SITE

After camp hunting trips through the South Shore district, Walter E. Burke, chairman of the camping committee, and Scout Executive W. E. Severance, found a splendid location for the summer camp which is to be conducted during the summer for the Boy Scouts of all parts of Quincy.

Troop 2, Watertown, 1917. Troop 2, Watertown prepares to march in a parade. (Courtesy L.A. Jones, Milford, NH, whose grandfather is one of the Scouts in the photo.)

ANSWER THE CALL
January 4th 6th & 7th

WILL YOU DO YOUR PART?

STOP THIS

HEED THIS

$60,000⁰⁰ CAMPAIGN
Greater Boston Federation Boy Scouts of America

Make checks payable to Allan Forbes Treasurer State Street Trust Co. 33 State St Boston

Fund-Raising Campaign, Greater Boston Federation, 1919. The wholesome image of Boy Scouts was used to appeal to donors to help keep boys out of trouble and involved in Scouting.

Troop 7, Brookline, 1918. This Troop was sponsored by the Harvard Church (currently known as United Parish) in Brookline. The church was destroyed by a fire in 1931 and rebuilt on its current site. Note the camping equipment: bed rolls, canteens, rucksacks, and fishing creels. The Scouts uniforms consisted of a buttoned jacket, trousers, leather or canvas leggings, and a flat-brimmed hat. Also note that the Scouts merit badges were sewn on the sleeves (see Scout sitting on far right in front row). (Courtesy: Collection of Elizabeth Aykroyd whose father Leonard Rhodes and cousin Sidney Johnson are in this photo)

Eagle Scout certificate, Logan LaMarche, 1919. Logan LaMarche of Troop 2 in Cambridge earned his first merit badge for Personal Health in 1914. Over the next 5 years, he earned badges in Swimming

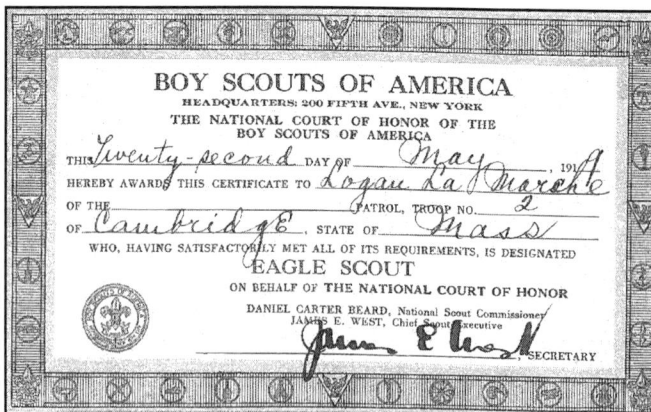

(1915), Automobiling (1916), and Surveying (1919). To earn Eagle rank in 1919, a Scout had to earn 21 merit badges: athletics or personal development, bird study, camping, civics, cooking, first aid, life saving, personal health, pathfinding, pioneering, and any ten others. (Courtesy: LaMarche estate)

20

1920

We're Going Camping!

In the Boston area, Scouting continued to be an attractive activity for boys. Numbers of troops increased in every town. Boys eagerly earned merit badges and went on camping trips. Community leaders petitioned to support Scouting. Just 10 years after its official start in the United States, Scouting was growing strong.

The 1920's saw many new camps formed around Boston. These camps provided real outdoor experiences that were still accessible in an era when many people relied on streetcars to get around. New Councils were formed in Cambridge (1923) and Sachem (1926) to help organize all the new troops being formed. This decade is best described as one of growth and excitement about Scouting.

Troop 5, Medford, Circa 1925. While some of the Scouts are standing at attention, the camera managed to capture a few of the more high-spirited Scouts making a human pyramid. Not much has changed.... (Courtesy: Private Collection)

Camp Massasoit, Plymouth, 1925. "Getting a Cold Drink." These Scouts were probably from the Quincy Council, which operated the camp on Long Pond in Plymouth in the early 1920's. On July 17, 1927, the Council formed the second (and current) Camp Massasoit on Elbow Pond in Plymouth.

Camp Massasoit, Plymouth, 1924. Camp Massasoit was one of the first camps established by the Quincy Council. The camp was conveniently located in Plymouth on Long Pond which gave campers the chance to boat and swim. This photo shows the "evening retreat."

Camp Massasoit, Plymouth, 1925. Boating at Camp Massasoit on Long Pond was a much-anticipated fun activity for campers. Note that these campers are not wearing life vests (PFDs) and are attired in their full uniforms rather than bathing suits.

Loon Pond Camp, 1927. Scouts could practically roll out of their cots and into the pond. The birch-tree sign reads "NAVY." The camp was located in Lakeville. It later became the Ted Williams Camp in 1958 before being acquired by the Town of Lakeville in 1986.

Troop 7, West Newton, 1923. A camping trip to unknown location. Note the jury-rigged cart (left, behind car) which must have served as a trailer to haul camping gear. (Courtesy: Private Collection)

Color Guard, Quincy, 1926. Note the two Sea Scouts on the right. Sea Scouts were founded in the United States in 1912, in Waltham, Massachusetts, by Arthur A. Carey aboard the schooner Pioneer. In 1913, the United States Navy recognized the importance of the program and encouraged its continuation and expansion. Sea Scouts continued with modest expansion up through WWII when nearly 27,000 Sea Scouts assisted and served in the Navy, impressing even the formidable Admiral Nimitz. Sea Scouts continued to be an all-male organization until 1972 when young women were invited to join.

Troop 1, East Boston, 1923. This photo was taken of the Troop 1 campsite at Camp Cobbett in Windham, NH. Little is known of this camp. There is a Cobbett Pond in Windham, so the Troop might have received permission from the owner of the land for a summer camping trip. (Courtesy: Private Collection)

Troop 11, Quincy, 1924. This photo was taken during the 4th week of summer camp at the first Camp Massasoit on Long Pond in Plymouth. Archie Briggs (white shirt, seated front) was the long-time Scoutmaster of Troop 11. In this photo: Front: Campbell, Nowell, Murray, Hall, Royner, Briggs, Abell. Back: Bassett, Burke, Campbell, and Hussey.

Scoutland - Camp Storrow - Hale Reservation

Starting about 1915, Boston Scout philanthropist Robert Seaver Hale began acquiring land on the Westwood/Dover line with the aim of creating a camp. On April 19, 1926 Camp Storrow was formed on this 20-acre parcel. This camp was named in honor of James Storrow, Boston philanthropist and National President of Boy Scouts 1925-1926. Over the next four years, a brook was dammed to make Storrow Pond, additional acreage was acquired, and a log cabin with a fireplace was built to serve as headquarters (burned, date unknown). In 1930, the camp was renamed Scoutland. Following death of Hale in 1941, Scoutland was renamed Hale Reservation in his honor.

Camp Storrow, Storrow Pond, Circa 1928.

Camp Storrow, Archery, 1927

Scoutland cabin, Circa 1930. Hale encouraged Scout troops to build their own cabins at Scoutland. From 1930 through the 1950's at least 30 troops built cabins. Few cabins remain, having fallen victim to neglect and weather.

Newspaper Story, Scoutland, 1930. The caption reads: Members of Boston Boy Scout Council on visit "Scoutland" and "Karlstein" Top photo, Councilors lunching A-la-Scout in Dover, Left to right-Richmond Mayo-Smith, George B. Morrison, Edward W. Welch, Robert S. Hale, Sewell C. Brackett, George F. Eddy. Bottom left, cutting a hole in the ice of the Charles River for a wash basin. Photo shows, Left to right, Alfred Washman, Clarence Bergstron. Bottom, right. George W. Austin, camping director for the Boston Scouts, summoning the councilors to "eats." Karlstein was a camp in Dover near Westwood and Dedham on the Charles River. It was operated by the Boston Council for a few years in the 1930's before Loon Pond Camp opened.

BOY SCOUT COUNCILORS INSPECT CAMPS SCOUTLAND AND KARLSTEIN

Greater Boston Executives Hosts on Visit to Dover and Dedham — Business Men Present Tin Plates For Appetizing Meal

Readville, 1921. Tenderfoot William J. Turner and his prize birdhouse.

Quincy Scouts, Boston Common, 1925. Photo taken near the baseball field in the north west part of the Common.

Troop 8, Arlington, 1927. This photo illustrates how the uniform was changing. Scouts were wearing (colorful) knee-high socks instead of leggings, "Sneex" sneakers, and neckerchiefs. (Sneex were made right at the Cambridge Rubber Company.) Badges were also moving from the sleeves to sashes. Photo taken on the steps of the Pleasant Street Congregational Church, Arlington, the troop sponsor. (Courtesy: Robbins Library, Arlington, MA)

1930

The First 25 Years

In 1935, Scouting celebrated its 25th Anniversary. In that time, Scouting was changing to meet the needs of boys. After nearly a decade of study and testing at select Councils, "Cubbing" began in 1933 to allow younger boys to get involved in Scouting (name was changed to Cub Scouts in 1945).

In the Boston area, camps were added. With the social upheaval of the Great Depression, Scouting was a way to keep youth active and safe in the wholesome structure of the Boy Scout program.

O. A. Kitterman

"Do a Good Turn Daily," Circa 1930. The ideals of Scouting resonated with Depression-era America. These Scouts are working to clear brush and weeds around the base of the Bunker Hill Monument in Charlestown. This photo was part of an article written by Oscar Avery (O. A.) Kitterman for Outdoor Life magazine extolling the virtues of Scouting. Kitterman became Scout Executive in Boston in 1930 after serving in similar positions in Kansas and Texas. He attended the World Jamboree in Holland in 1937 and served in Boston until 1945.

Camp Sachem, Chickagami Site, Circa 1935. This idyllic waterfront camp site features platform tents just steps from a tidy beach on Gregg Lake in Antrim, NH. Canoes (right) were available for the Scouts. (Courtesy: Private Collection)

Troop 306, Arlington, 1937. These Scouts and their Scoutmasters are in front of the Ballard Cabin at Camp Sachem during the summer of 1937.

Camp Sachem, 1938. Boating and canoeing was always a popular activity at Scout camps. Gregg Lake was the perfect spot to explore via canoe. (Courtesy: Private Collection)

Camp Sachem, Ferry, 1930. This was the only way to the camp when it was first founded in 1928. A road into the camp was not built until 1933. (Courtesy: Private Collection)

Camp Massasoit, Rowing, 1931. Note the swim platform further out in the water, complete with a high diving board.

Camp Massasoit, Washing Dishes, 1932. These Quincy Scouts lifted bins of dishes into pots of boiling water to clean and sterilize the dishes. No dishwashers here!

Camp Manning, Waterfront, 1935. Camp Manning was located in Andover, MA. It was operated by the Malden Council. Scouts had a waterfront on Pomp's Pond with boats and a swim platform with a slide. (back center) (Courtesy: Andover Historical Society)

Troop 11, Quincy, 1932. These Scouts are at summer camp at Camp Massasoit in Plymouth. Note that they are wearing the newer style uniforms which began to be introduced in the late 1920's.

Camp Manning, Mess Call, 1935. Campers line up for lunch at Camp Manning. The dining hall (lower left) remains today as part of the public park at Pomp's Pond in Andover, MA. (Courtesy: Andover Historical Society)

Camp Kenoza

CONDUCTED BY THE

Medford Council, Inc.,

Boy Scouts of America

Comprising Burlington, Medford, Stoneham
Winchester, Woburn

Season 1931

June 27 to August 22

Scout Office, Medford
Medford Building, Medford Square
Phone Mystic 4292

Camp Office
Coombs Corner, Amesbury
Phone, 1172-6

Program

Camp Kenoza will be brimful of activity with something to do, something to think about, something to enjoy from reveille to taps every day. Special attention will be given to scouts who cannot swim. Test cards should be taken to camp. Every scout should advance in rank during his stay in camp.

7:00	First Call.
7:05	Reveille. Morning Dip, (optional). Wash and Dress.
7:55	Morning Colors. Tent Leaders Report.
8:00	Breakfast.
8:40	Service Details.
9:30	Inspection, Personal and Tent by Camp Leaders.

Where We Live

10:00	Assembly for Scoutcraft—A Scouts Opportunity to Advance.
11:45	Morning Swim—Buddy and Check System Used.
12:15	Recall.
1:00	Dinner.
1:45	Camp Store Open, Siesta, Campers Rest in Tents. Tent Leaders Report.
2:45	Recreational Period, Games, Athletics, Swimming Meets, Boat Races, Baseball, Craftwork, Archery, Boating.
5:00	Afternoon Swim.
5:40	Recall—Life Saving Crew Swim.
6:15	Supper.
7:15	Evening Colors, Evening Activities, Boating, Volley Ball.
8:15	Camp Fires, Dramatics, Stunt Nights.
9:15	Call to Quarters—Tent Leaders Report.
9:30	Tatoo.
9:40	Taps, Lights Out, Ten Hours, Refreshing Sleep.

Camp Kenoza, Brochure, 1931. Camp Kenoza in Amesbury, MA, was for Scouts from the Medford Council. Activities included swimming, volleyball, Scoutcraft, archery, and more. Note the schedule: Scouts were kept busy from 7:00 am until 9:30 pm with both organized activities and scheduled events. Camp Kenoza was renamed Camp Fellsland sometime after 1932 after the Fellsland Council was organized. The name - Kenoza - had frequently cause confusion. Kenoza Lake was in Haverhill but the camp was located in Amesbury. No one is sure why the Amesbury camp was named for a lake in Haverhill. (Courtesy: Private Collection)

Camp Massasoit, Waterfront, 1931. This was the second (and final) location for Camp Massasoit which moved to its current location in 1927.

Camp Quinapoxet, Campers Climbing Mount Washington, 1934. Camp Quinapoxet, operated by the Cambridge Council, was originally founded in 1925 on Lake Quinapoxet in Jefferson, MA. In 1926 and 1927, it was located in Charlton, MA. By 1928 it had moved to its present location on Hubbard Pond in Rindge, NH. In 2000, Camp Quinapoxet was sold to Massachusetts Audubon. They changed the name to Camp Wildwood and offer a nature-based program at that site.

Scout Uniform Advertisement, Jordan Marsh, 1932. Jordan Marsh was a shopping institution in Boston for over 100 years. The flagship store was on Washington Street at the present site of Downtown Crossing. Jordan Marsh was bought by Macy's in 1996. In 1933, Cub Scouts were the newest branch of Boy Scouts. Notice the shorts that the Scout is wearing. This was part of the new uniform which had both long trousers and shorts.

1940

The War Years

During WWII, Scouts played an important role in the home-front war effort. Scouts held scrap metal drives, collected rubber and paper, helped with medical brigades, and assisted with war bond drives. Sea Scouts served in the Navy, impressing even the formidable Admiral Nimitz with their training and preparedness. Young men who were Eagle Scouts one year might find themselves on the front line in Europe or in the Pacific the next. Even with the war going on, Boy Scouts of America was thriving. New Scout camps opened, new merit badges were introduced. There was a new emphasis on conservation and lower-impact outdoor activities. In 1946, Boy Scouts of America reached 2,000,000 members. In 1941, Sir Robert Baden-Powell died in Kenya. His grave is a national monument.

Locally, in 1949 Theodore Storer donated 2250 acres in Stafford NH to the Quannapowit Council of Boy Scouts. This tract would become Parker Mountain Scout Reservation.

Troop 103, Belmont, 1949. These Scouts are hiking in to Camp Oak, Bedford. MA. (Courtesy: Private Collection)

Camp Massasoit, Staff, 1947. This photo was taken in front of the totem pole which was right outside the camp director's office. (Photo and description of totem pole on page 42). The man dressed in Native American costume was probably going to portray Chief Massasoit, namesake of the camp. Since Boy Scouts began, Native American lore and rituals have been a respected part of Scouting. But in the 1940's, it was still common for Americans to hold stereotypical views of Native American customs and rituals. Outside of Boy Scouts, probably the only Native America figure most Scouts were exposed to was Tonto on The Lone Ranger. In the 1970's, with the help of Native American leaders and educators, Boy Scouts reviewed and updated their use of Native American customs and rituals so these traditions could continue to play the important role they have always played in Scouting, while respecting their cultural significance.

Camp Massasoit, Brochure, 1944. This shows an aerial view of Elbow Pond where the camp is located.

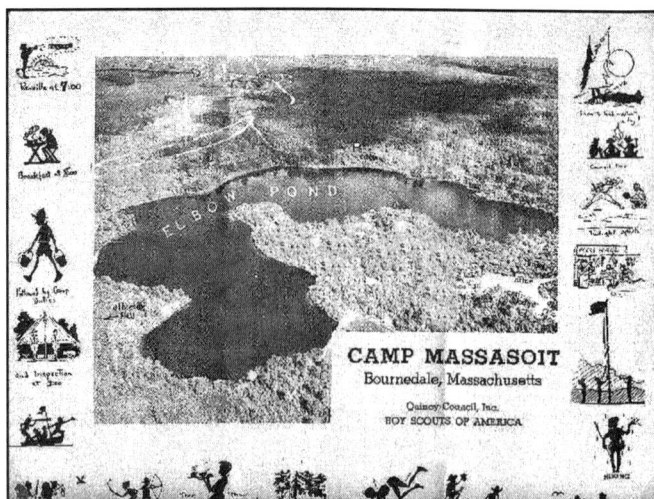

CAMP MASSASOIT
Bournedale, Massachusetts

Quincy Council, Inc.
BOY SCOUTS OF AMERICA

Camp Sachem, Waterfront, 1947. The waterfront is lined with parents leaning against the fence. It's probably parent's day where Scouts would show off their skills and hope mom brought a batch of home-baked treats to share with buddies. See another photo of the waterfront on page 56.

Camp Fellsland, Waterfront, 1940. Camp Fellsland was called Camp Kenoza until shortly after 1932 when the camp was renamed for the new Fellsland Council which had been formed in 1931. Camp Fellsland/Kenoza was located on Tuxbury Pond in Amesbury, MA. Also on Tuxbury Pond was Camp Pow Wow, operated by the Lynn Council, and later the Bay Shore Council. (Courtesy: Private Collection)

Advertisement, Boy Scout Week, 1940. Caption reads: "When the Boy Scouts of America celebrates its 30th birthday on Thursday, February 8, all of the 1,330,000 Scouts, Cubs, and Scout leaders will re-dedicate themselves to the service motive which has characterized the Movement for three decades. Scouting offers adventure, fun, and achievement - attractive to all boys - through the democratic life of the Scout Troop and Patrol as essential ingredients in its character-influencing program for the boys of America. Drawing on the rich experience of the Movement, local and national Scout leaders anticipate the opportunity to serve more boys annually." (© Boy Scouts of America. Used by permission)

Advertisement, Boy Scout Week, 1945. Caption reads: "Boy Scouts of the United Nations are planning to resume their world-wide friendships through correspondence, exchange of equipment, and by meeting in person at the Great World Scout Jamborees when the war is won. The Boy Scouts of America, celebrating its 35th anniversary from February 8 - 14, with its theme "Scouts of the World - Brothers Together" is encouraging its members to establish contacts with other Scout troops in war-torn lands, and if possible, help them restore Scouting." While WWII was not over yet, the news from Europe was hopeful. The Allied forces were moving on Germany and an end to the war in Europe finally seemed to be in sight. But there is still uncertainty in the world in February 1945. The United States and its allies were gearing up for what was expected to be a long, bloody fight in the Pacific. (© Boy Scouts of America. Used by permission)

World-Wide Friendships

SCOUTS OF THE WORLD - BROTHERS TOGETHER

"Be Prepared"
BOY SCOUT WEEK
FEBRUARY 8TH-14TH 1945
THE 35TH ANNIVERSARY
OF THE
BOY SCOUTS OF AMERICA
Over 1,800,000 Members

Advertisement, Boy Scout Week, 1948. The war is over. There is a renewed sense of optimism and pride. Notice that the uniform hat (field cap) resembles a military cap. The field cap became the standard uniform hat in 1943. Compare with the advertisement (left) from 1940. (© Boy Scouts of America. Used by permission)

The Scout Citizen at Work
...IN HIS HOME
...IN HIS COMMUNITY
...IN HIS NATION
...IN HIS WORLD

Thirty-Eighth Anniversary
BOY SCOUT WEEK
FEBRUARY 6TH TO 12TH

41

Camp Massasoit, Totem Pole, 1940. This totem pole was located right outside the camp director's office. It was carved and designed by Charlie Perkins, Assistant Scoutmaster Troop 4 (town unknown) who also served as Assistant Waterfront Director at the camp. The totem pole depicts (bottom to top) a blue salamander, a bright orange Beelzebub, and a bird with a skull for a head. Pictured are Scouts (left) Eaton Elz and John Pitts.

Troop 6, Quincy, 1949. These Scouts were part of the Quincy Council campout in the Blue Hills in June 1949. This Troop was sponsored by the Hough's Neck Congregational Church. (Left) Roger McDermott, Fred Lucas, William Bonnyman, Walter Morse, Larry Shaw. Standing; Patrol Leader Scott McKay.

Loon Pond Camp, Lakeville, Circa 1945. The camp was operated by the Boston Council and located in Lakeville, MA. It later became the Ted Williams Camp in 1958 before being acquired by the Town of Lakeville in 1986.

Rover Scouts, Quincy, 1947. Scouts could build their own cabins at the "Uncle Rufus Memorial Camp" on the shores of Ponkapoag Pond in Canton, MA. "Uncle Rufus" was Rufus Poole, a long-time Scouter in the Quincy Council. Called the "Rover Cabin," it was for use of Rover and Senior Scouts in Quincy. The Rovers cut the logs, built the cabin and were in process of installing the doors and windows and building a fireplace when this photo was taken. In the picture are (left to right) Myron Lineman, Roland W. Parsons, and William J. V. Babcock. Some of these cabins are currently used as part of the Appalachian Mountain Club (AMC) campsite.

Ship 9, 1946. Sea Scouts receive their charter on February 11, 1946. Front row (Left) David Cobb, Clifford O. Mason (Troop Chairman, presenting award), Skipper John R. Nelson, and Daniel Page. Middle row: Norman Ellis, Richard Howard, Mate Robert Sherman, William Mullin, Alden Powers, and James Holland. Back row: Donald Chapman, Ronald Weir, Paul Collins, and Arthur Porter, Jr.

Quincy, Eagle Scouts, 1941. While the identity of these Scouts is not known, what is interesting is that the Scout on the left is wearing the old style uniform while the Scout on the right is wearing the new style uniform.

1950

Optimism and Growth

The 1950's were an exciting period of growth for Boy Scouts both locally and nationally. In 1950, the U.S. Post Office issued its first official Boy Scout stamp. In 1951, Scouts across the country "Do a Good Turn" and collect 2,000,000 pounds of clothing for war relief efforts. Scouts participated in community Civil Defense and get-out-the-vote efforts. Scouting reached a milestone of 5,000,000 Scouts in 1959 the United States.

Locally, Boston Minuteman Council was expanding its camping options. Newly acquired Parker Mountain Scout Reservation was soon joined by T.L. Storer Scout Reservation and Camp Sayre. Adams Pond Camp was dedicated July 18, 1958 with "accommodations for 550 campers." New Hampshire Governor Lane Dwinell gave the keynote address at the dedication. Boston Council of Boy Scouts had 17,500 registered Scouts.

Loon Pond Camp, Retreat, 1950.

"Get in on" THE NATIONAL JAMBOREE

VALLEY FORGE, PA.
JUNE 30th – JULY 6th, 1950
40th ANNIVERSARY CRUSADE – BOY SCOUTS OF AMERICA

National Scout Jamboree, Valley Forge, PA, 1950. The first national Jamboree was scheduled for 1935 to celebrate the 25th anniversary of Scouting, but was delayed by the polio epidemic until 1937. About 25,000 Scouts camped on the National Mall and the Tidal Basin in Washington, DC. WWII halted any further National Jamborees, so the first Jamboree held after the end of the war was in 1950. Since then, national jamborees have been held approximately every 4 years. Since 1981, the jamboree has been held at Fort A.P. Hill in Virginia. 2010 will be the last jamboree held at Fort A.P. Hill. The location for the 2013 jamboree has not been decided. (© Boy Scouts of America. Used by permission)

Possibly Troop 4, Dorchester, Rifle Range, Circa 1950.

If these Scouts were working on a shooting merit badge, it would have been the Marksmanship badge. When the merit badge was first introduced in 1910, it was called Marksman Badge. It was renamed in 1911 to Marksmanship Badge.

Troop 103, Belmont, 1953. Troop 103 was camping at a Sachem Council Camporee at Camp Oak in Bedford. Camp Oak, in Bedford, MA, was a short-term camp operated by the Sachem Council. The camp was located on the Middlesex Turnpike on the Shawsheen River. In addition to camp sites, troops of the Council could have their own sites and build cabins. Camp Oak no longer exists. Oak Office Park in Bedford, MA, is now located on the site of the former camp. See Oak Camp sign on page 96. (Courtesy: Private Collection)

Camp Sachem, Nikiwigi Campfire Selection Ceremony, Circa 1950. Honor societies started in Pennsylvania in 1915 and spread to other northeastern camps. Order of the Arrow (OA) is the best know of these societies. But at a few camps, there were alternative societies. The Order of Nikiwigi (or Tribe of Nikiwigi) was at three camps in New England beginning in the 1930's, one in Maine, one in Massachusetts, and at Camp Sachem. There were three rank levels: Ranger, Order of the Trail, and Nikiwigi. Scouts received a leather pouch to wear around their neck with their uniform. While OA displaced Nikiwigi at the other two camps in the 1940's, Nikiwigi lasted at Camp Sachem until the 1960's.

47

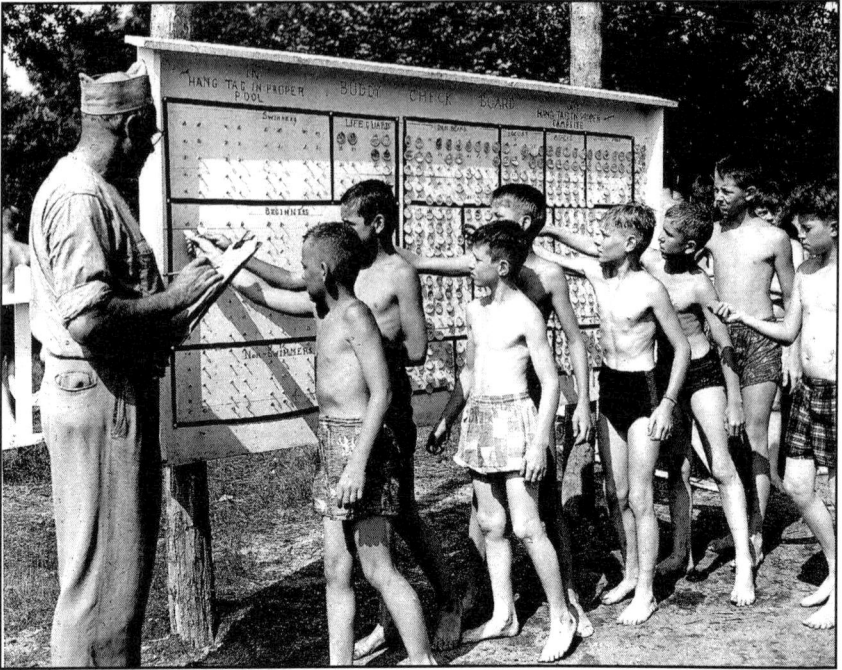

Loon Pond Camp, Lakeville, 1951. The "Buddy Board" at the waterfront helped to assure that every Scout was safe and accounted for while swimming.

Loon Pond Camp, Lakeville, 1950. The waterfront was one of the most popular areas at any camp. Through the trees in the center of the photo, you can just see the life guard station and to the left of that the docks at the swimming beach.

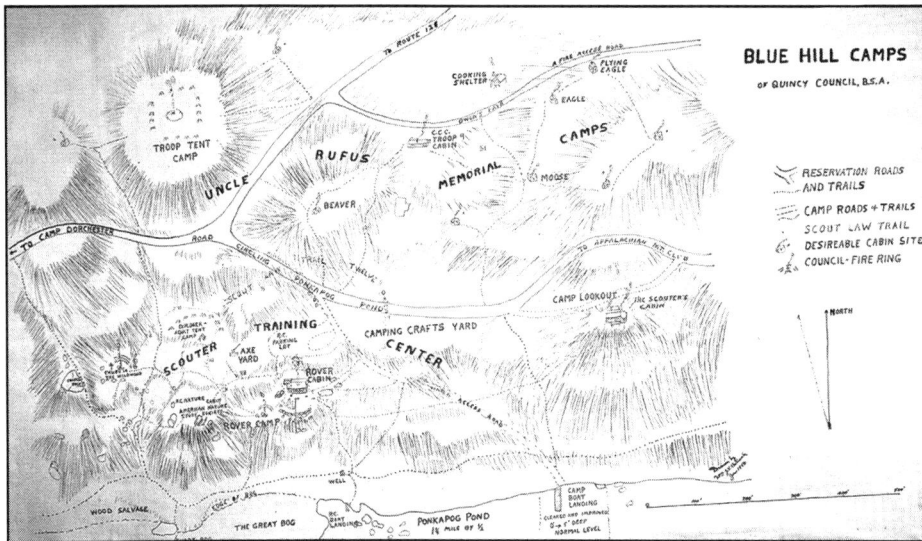

Blue Hill Camp, Map, Circa 1955. Scouts could build their own cabins at the "Uncle Rufus Memorial Camp" on the shores of Ponkapoag Pond in Canton, MA. "Uncle Rufus" was Rufus Poole, a long-time Scouter in the Quincy Council. This site is in the Blue Hills reservation and some of it is currently used as part of the Appalachian Mountain Club (AMC) campsite.

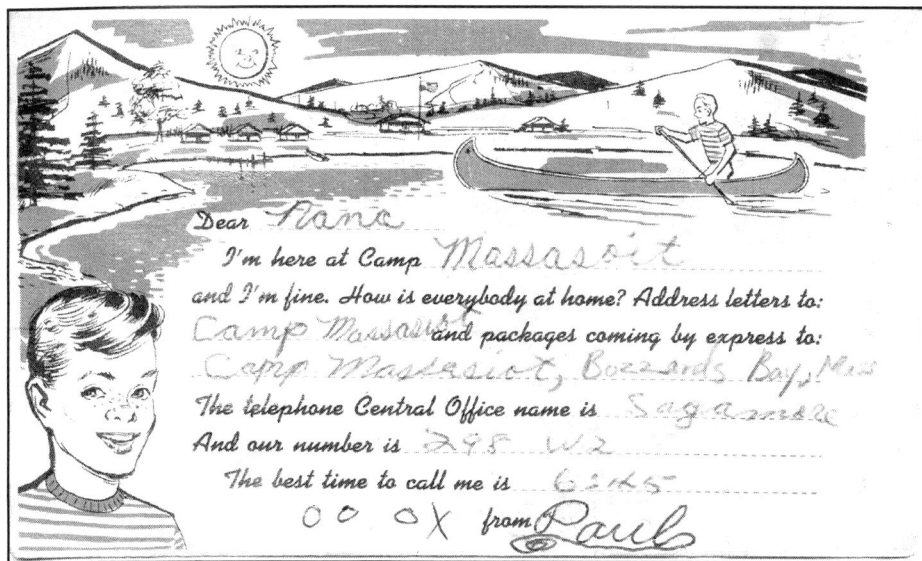

Camp Massasoit, Postcard, 1957. Letters home from camp don't get much easier than this fill-in-the-blank card supplied by the camp. But Paul did remember to add hugs and kisses (0 0 0 X) for his Nana.

49

Camp Sayre, Milton, Cabin, 1952. On October 19, 1952, Boston Council of Boy Scouts dedicated their newest camp, Camp Sayre. Camp Sayre is located in the Blue Hills Reservation, on Unquity Road in Milton, MA. The camp consists of 100 acres donated by Mr. and Mrs. Elliot Henderson. The camp was named in honor of their son, David Sayre Henderson who died in 1941 at age 16. Mr. Henderson was a Vice President of the Council. Construction costs were largely covered by a grant from the Charles Hayden Foundation. There were three tent-camping areas and five cabin sites to accommodate Scouts. A large hall was also built to accommodate up to 100 Scouts and leaders for training programs. Camp Sayre is site of the Egan Center which is the current headquarters for Boston Minuteman Council.

Camp Sayre, Milton, Winter Hike, 1953. This photo was part of a promotional advertisement by the Old Colony Trust Company. The advertisement compared the growth and changes of Scouting to life changes that one should prepare for.

Camp Quinapoxet, 25th Anniversary, 1953. Celebrating the 25th Anniversary of Camp Quinapoxet are: Front: two unknown Order of the Arrow Scouts dressed in Native American costumes.

Back: (Left) Ted Storer, Joe DeGuglielmo, and Mayor Edward Crane. Man on far right may be Frank Baldwin.

Troop 15, Melrose, Circa 1955. Troop 15 on a camping trip at an unknown location (could be Camp Fellsland). Note that the American flag has 48 stars.

Camp Sachem, Totem Pole, 1954. Totem poles were a common sight at Scout camps. Native American symbols and names were often incorporated into Boy Scouts. (Courtesy: Private Collection)

1960

50 Years of Scouting

The 1960's were a decade of change. The beginning of the 1960's was marked by the optimism of the Kennedy election and the excitement of the space program. It was also marked by the social upheaval of the Vietnam war and the Civil Rights movement. The country was changing - and so was Boy Scouts. The 1965 handbook included non-white boys in illustrations for the first time. In 1969, Eagle Scout Neil Armstrong became the first man to walk on the Moon.

Boy Scouts celebrated its 50th anniversary in 1960. There was a National Jamboree in Colorado and proclamations from President Kennedy (who was honored for a "mile swim" for his heroic efforts to save his crew when he was a PT boat skipper.) Locally, Boston Minuteman Council Scouts were keeping the traditions of Scouting: camping, community service, and rank advancement.

Quincy Scouts, National Jamboree, 1960.
(Left) Peter Rubin and Raymond Dunn attended the Fifth National Boy Scout Jamboree near Pike's Peak in Colorado Springs, CO. About 55,000 Scouts attended this event.

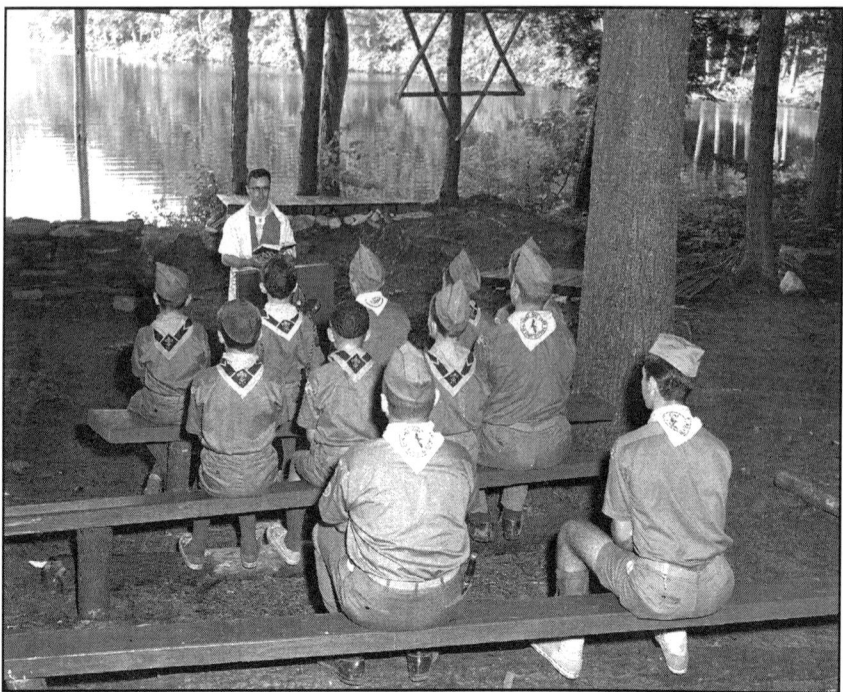

Wild Goose Camp-Adams Pond Camp, Religious Services, 1967.
Scouts were encouraged to attend services in their faith. The outdoor
settings made services memorable for many campers.

MAY 4-5, 1962 | BOSTON GARDEN
NORTH STATION – BOSTON, MASS.

SCOUT CAPADES

MAY 4 – 8 P.M.
MAY 5 – 1:30 and 8 P.M.

Presented by
Boston and Cambridge Councils
BOY SCOUTS OF AMERICA

SCOUT CAPADES ...for the whole family!

Scout Capades Program, 1962. In the early 1960's, Councils all over the country held Scout Capades. Part talent show, part Scouting skills demonstration, and part old-fashioned rally, these shows routinely attracted thousands of Scouts and spectators. Reports around the country of other Scout Capades talk about Native American dancing, fire building contests, and sled races. There were even Scout Snow-Capades which seem to be a bigger version of a Klondike Derby. The Boston Scout Capades were jointly sponsored by the Boston and Cambridge Councils and held at the old Boston Garden.

Troop 306, Arlington, Insignia, 1967. Before 1972, this was the common shoulder insignia: town name, state underneath, 1-3 digits for your troop number, and a patrol or leadership patch. This insignia also includes a gold bar signifying a troop which has been chartered for 50+ years (silver bar for 25+ years). This troop also had a coordinating neckerchief. In 1972. BSA overhauled all the designs for merit badges and CSPs and made them colorful and attractive. Units began choosing to wear the new CSPs instead of the old red-and-white town insignia.

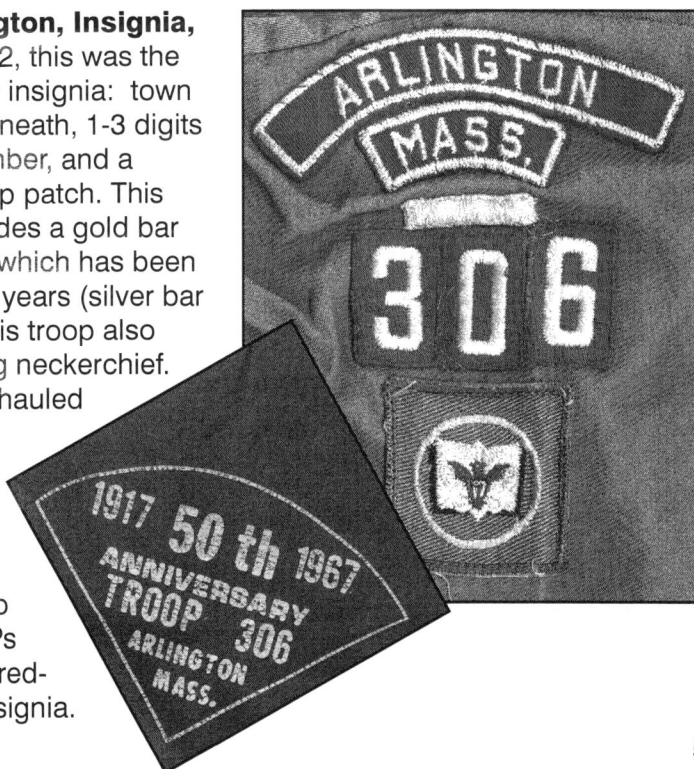

Archery, 1967. While we don't know the identity of the Scouts, what's interesting to note is the traditional-style bows.

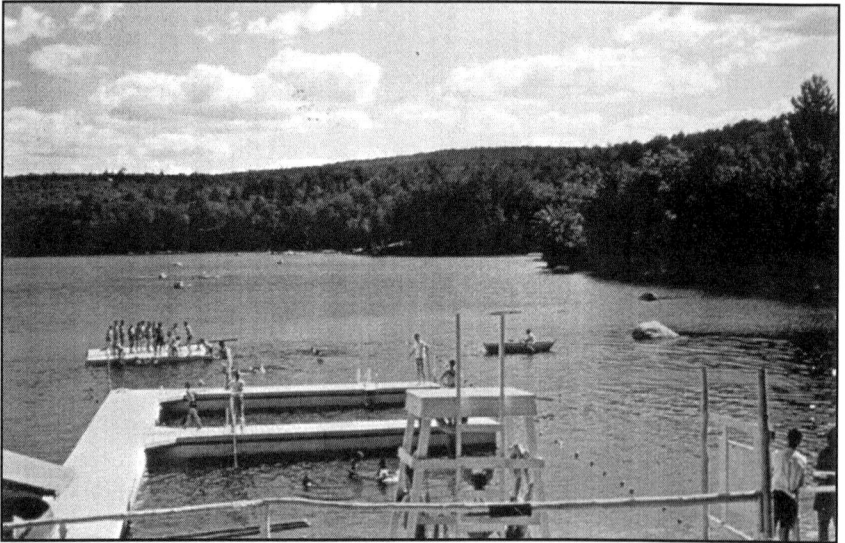

Camp Sachem, Waterfront, 1962. This was the swimming area on Gregg Lake including docks and a swim platform with a diving board. Far out on the lake, there are about a dozen canoes and boats. (Courtesy: Private Collection)

Troop 401, Medford, 1969. Scout Troop 401 was camping at Parker Mountain when this photo was taken. The older Scouts on the left are hamming it up for the camera. (Courtesy: Private Collection)

Parker Mountain Scout Reservation, Waterfront, 1962. This photo, taken from a boat on Big Willey Pond, shows the swim platform (right) and the beach and docks (rear). Look closely and you can see a Scout mid-dive from the swim platform.

Jamboree Troop, Boston Council, 1964. This Troop traveled to the Valley Forge National Jamboree in July 1964.On their return trip, they stopped in New York to visit the World's Fair. (Courtesy: Trustees of Boston Public Library)

Silver Beaver Award, 1967. The Silver Beaver Award is presented to Scouters (adult leaders and volunteers) for outstanding service to Scouting. This ceremony took place at Valle's Steakhouse in Saugus, MA in February, 1967. (Left) Council Chairman Charles Burke (Watertown)

presented award to: Malcom Gavin (Lexington), H. Andrew Brodecki (Reading), Ernest Lay (Melrose), and Council President John Mugar (Belmont).

Quincy Scouts, 1960. These two Scouts on the left are members of Order of the Arrow (OA) as shown by their white sashes. Read more about the history of the OA on page 83.

Eagle Scouts, State House, 1960. Eagle Scouts attended the 50th annual reception at the State House, Boston, hosted by Governor Furcolo. Front row (left): John Gallant (Arlington), Alan McDougal (Winchester), George Crowley (Quincy), Peter Kilmartin (Concord), Bruce Owen (Holden), Back row (left): Harry Ramsey (Wachusett), Richard Lavoie (New Bedford), Glenn Gulezian (Haverhill), Robert Biza (Agawam), Leon Berman (Chelsea).

Advertisement, 1960. Fiftieth Anniversary pot luck dinner program cover. This dinner was held at the Commonwealth Armory on May 11, 1961.

Poster, 50th Anniversary, 1960. This poster features the iconic Scouting statue sculpted by Dr. R. Tait McKenzie in 1915. Dr. McKenzie was a member of the Philadelphia Council Executive Board from 1911-1938. The models were Asa Franklin Hooven and G. Dunbar Shewell.

Ten 18-inch bronze copies were cast and presented to Sir Robert Baden-Powell and Charles Lindbergh among others. Beginning in 1917, plaster copies were made and distributed by the National Council. In 1934 an 8-inch metal copy, finished in bronze or silver, was made by the National Council. In 1950, a 4-inch "desk-size" was added.

BOY SCOUTS OF AMERICA

1910 1960

BE PREPARED

50 YEARS OF SERVICE

In 1937, the Philadelphia Council moved its office and wanted a life-size casting of the statue. Since the original models were now adults, McKenzie chose four other Scouts to serve as the new models. Since that time, about 50 copies have been cast and installed throughout the United States - and one in Gillwell in Great Britain.
(© Boy Scouts of America. Used by permission)

1970

Patriotism and Pride

In the 1970's, the United States prepared for its bicentennial celebration in 1976. Boy Scouts of America joined in the celebration by holding a massive Scout skills demonstration on the Mall in Washington, DC. Twelve Scouts met with President Gerald Ford (who was an Eagle Scout) and delivered a Report to the Nation. Nationally, the numbers of boys who were joining Scouts was dropping. BSA launched several campaigns to increase interest and membership. In 1976, Norman Rockwell's iconic Boy Scout illustrations toured the nation.

Locally, Camp Massasoit quietly closed in 1977, but dedicated volunteers raised money to refurbish and reopen the camp in 1979. An article in a 1979 Boston Minuteman Council newsletter talks about Scouts learning how to use computers by keypunching cards to create computer programs. Scouting was changing with the times to stay relevant to boys.

Parker Mountain Scout Reservation, Retreat, 1974. Scouts taking part in evening retreat.

Camp Sachem, Canoeing, Circa 1975. Waterfront activities have always been a highlight at Camp Sachem on Gregg Lake in Antrim, NH. (Courtesy: Trustees of Boston Public Library)

Camp Sachem, Rowboats, 1971. This was probably visiting day as the Scouts are in full uniform. In the background is Magee Boat House and further up the hill through the trees is Chickagami Cabin. See photo of site from 1930's on page 30. (Courtesy: Trustees of Boston Public Library)

T.L. Storer Scout Reservation, Rifle Range, Circa 1975. Shooting sports are always very popular. Scouts learn gun safety, marksmanship, and get instruction. This range was a huge improvement over the previous site.

Camp Sachem, Webelos, 1978. Webelos learn to paddle their canoe during Webelos Week at Camp Sachem in 1978. Building at center on shore is camp trading post. (Courtesy: Private Collection)

Probably T.L. Storer Scout Reservation, Ropes Challenge, 1976.
During the 1970's, challenge courses with ropes and climbing became
very popular activities at camps. These Scouts are climbing across a
rope bridge.

T.L. Storer Scout Reservation, Circa 1975. These Scouts are well-
prepared with loaded backpacks. This sign is at the entrance to the
camp.

Camp Sachem, Retreat, 1978. Webelos from Arlington Cub Pack at Webelos Week performing the evening retreat. (Courtesy: Private Collection)

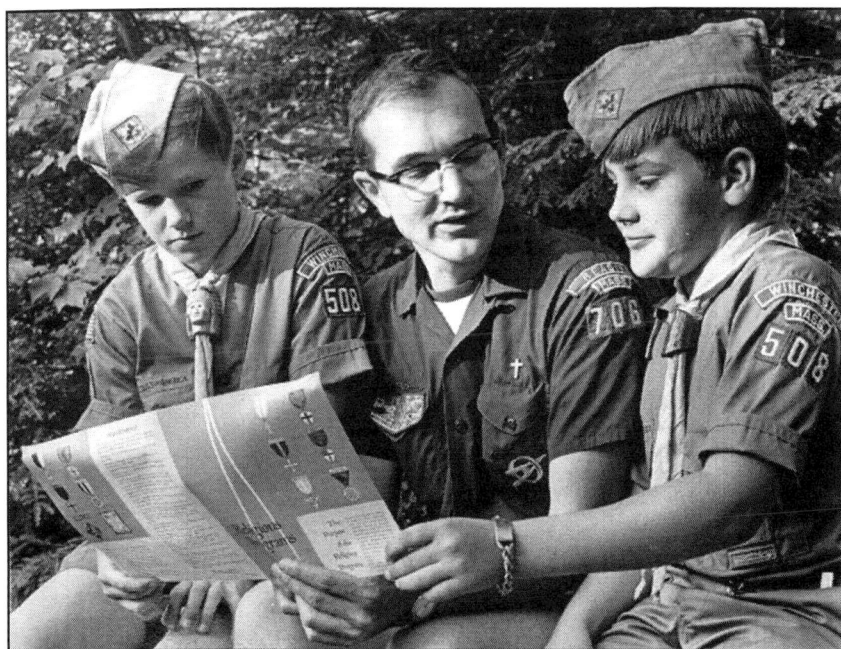

Troop 508, Winchester; Troop 706, Reading, Circa 1975. These Scouts from Troop 508, Winchester, MA, are talking with a chaplain from Troop 706 in Reading, MA, about the religious medals which can be earned by Scouts. (Courtesy: Trustees of Boston Public Library)

Camp Massasoit, Renovations, 1979. In 1977, Camp Massasoit was closed. For two years, the Boston Minuteman Council attempted to sell the site. In 1979, dedicated volunteers began raising funds with the aim of saving the camp. With $18,000 in cash donations and $12,000 worth of labor donations, the camp was refurbished and returned to use. In this photo, Mark Shotte, Troop 15, Quincy, helps install insulation in the administration building.

T.L. Storer Scout Reservation Dining Hall, Circa 1975. The dining hall at T.L. Storer looks very much the same today as it did in the 1970's. Even the benches and tables in this photo are still in use today.

Cardinal Cushing, Ad Altare Dei award, 1970. In February 1970, Cardinal Richard Cushing presented the Ad Altare Dei award to 237 Scouts at the Cathedral of the Holy Cross in Boston. The Ad Altare Dei is a Roman Catholic Boy Scout award. Cardinal Cushing is on the left side, sitting at the front of the line of Scouts. (Courtesy: Trustees of Boston Public Library)

Camp Quinapoxet

50th Anniversary

1925-1975

Cambridge Council, BSA

Camp Quinapoxet, 50th Anniversary, 1975. Camp Quinapoxet, operated by the Cambridge Council, was originally founded in 1925 on Lake Quinapoxet in Jefferson, MA. In 1926 and 1927, it was located in Charlton, MA. By 1928 it had moved to its present location on Hubbard Pond in Rindge, NH. In 2000, Camp Quinapoxet was sold to Massachusetts Audubon who changed the name to Camp Wildwood. Massachusetts Audubon continues to run a nature-based program at that camp.

Silver Fawn Award, 1971. The Silver Fawn award was presented to outstanding women volunteers in Scouting. It was first awarded in 1971. In this photo Mary Mahony (left) and Ruth Famolari received the award from a Scout from Troop 28, Dorchester. The Silver Fawn was equal to the Silver Beaver award given to male Scout volunteers. After 1974, the Silver Fawn was discontinued when the decision was made to present the Silver Beaver to any Scout volunteer - male or female - who make outstanding contributions to Scouting. (Courtesy: Trustees of Boston Public Library)

Silver Beaver
and
Silver Fawn Awards

PRESENTED BY

MINUTEMAN COUNCIL, INC.
BOY SCOUTS OF AMERICA
January 28, 1974

1980

Rebuilding

Because Scouting membership declined in the 1970's, the 1980's were about rebuilding. In 1982, Tiger Cubs for first graders and Varsity Scouting began. Scouting registered its 1,000,000th Eagle Scout. In 1985, Boy Scouts of America celebrated its 75th anniversary. There were 5,000,000 active Boy Scouts in the United States by 1986. Also in 1986, the Scouting for Food program began to help stock the nation's food pantries. Boy Scouts of America voted in 1988 to officially open leadership positions to women.

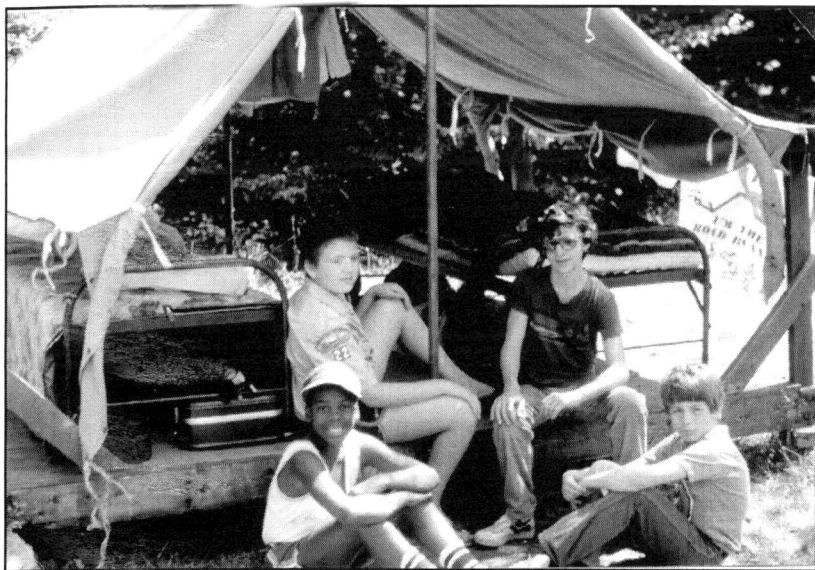

Scouts at Camp, 1983. The Scout seated in the back on the left is from Troop 22 (perhaps North Bay Council). The flag on the right reads "I'm the Road Runner."

Wild Goose Camp, Waterfront, 1982. Compare this to the Buddy Board photo from 1951 from Loon Pond Camp on page 48.

T.L. Storer Scout Reservation, Waterfront, 1981. Rowing on the pond is always one of the most anticipated activities at camp. This was as true in the 1980's as it was in earlier decades. Compare this photo with the one from 1925 at Camp Massasoit on page 23 or the photo from Loon Pond Camp from 1950 on page 48.

Adams Pond Camp, Totem Pole and Campfire Ring, 1985. This was a much-beloved location at the camp, site of many gatherings.

T.L. Storer Scout Reservation, Waterfront, 1981. Scouts rowing canoes and using Sailfish sailboat.

Troop 401, Wakefield, Winter Camping, 1982. Scouts are camping at Breakheart Reservation in Saugus, MA. Note that the Scouts are all wearing ice skates. (Courtesy: Private Collection)

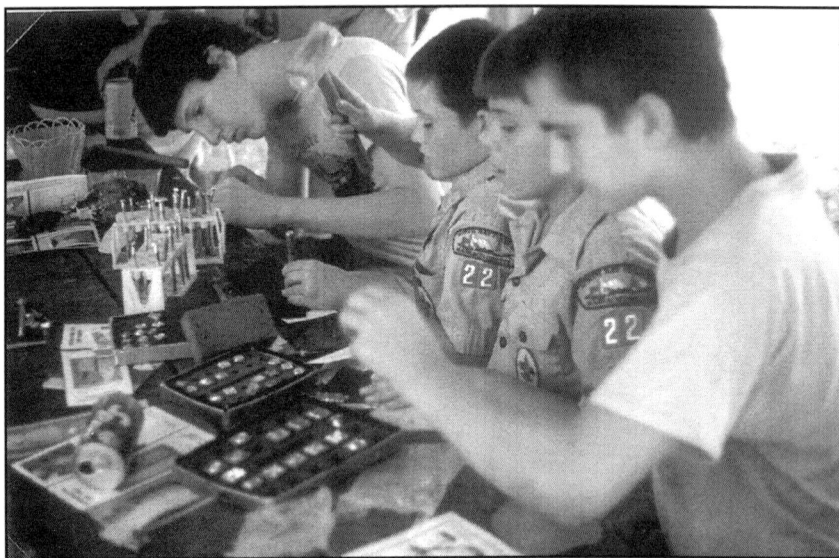

Probably T.L. Storer Scout Reservation, Scoutcraft, 1983. Scoutcraft is always a popular activity at camp. Scouts here are stamping and carving leather and making baskets.The Scouts in uniform are from Troop 22 of the North Bay Council, now part of Yankee Clipper Council.

Parker Mountain Scout Reservation, Archery, 1982.

Parker Mountain Scout Reservation, Rifle Range, 1982. Scouts learn gun safety, marksmanship, and receive instruction to improve their skill. Obviously this was a posed photo as the Scouts are aiming directly at the photographer!

Troop 2, Dedham, 1982. It was traditional up through the 1980's for Troops to have a group photo taken at camp. Boston Minuteman archives have hundreds of copies of Troop photos in our files. This photo was taken at Wild Goose Camp, Barnstead, NH.

Pinewood Derby, Metacom District, 1982. Cub Scouts hold an annual Pinewood Derby where they build and race wooden cars. Winners in each Pack compete at the district level. The Metacom District Pinewood race was held on April 3, 1982 at the Islington Church in Westwood, MA. (Left) First Place, Michael Spalding, Islington Pack 1; Second Place, Kevin McGeachie, Needham Pack 4; Third Place, Greg Everett, Dedham Pack 1. Read about the history of the Pinewood Derby on page 78.

Probably T.L. Storer Scout Reservation, Campfire, 1982. These Scouts may be from Melrose, troop unknown, enjoying one of the traditions of camp: a huge bonfire with stories, skits, and camp songs.

T.L. Storer Scout Reservation, Flag ceremony, 1982. Scouts begin and end every day at camp with a formal flag raising and lowering ceremony.

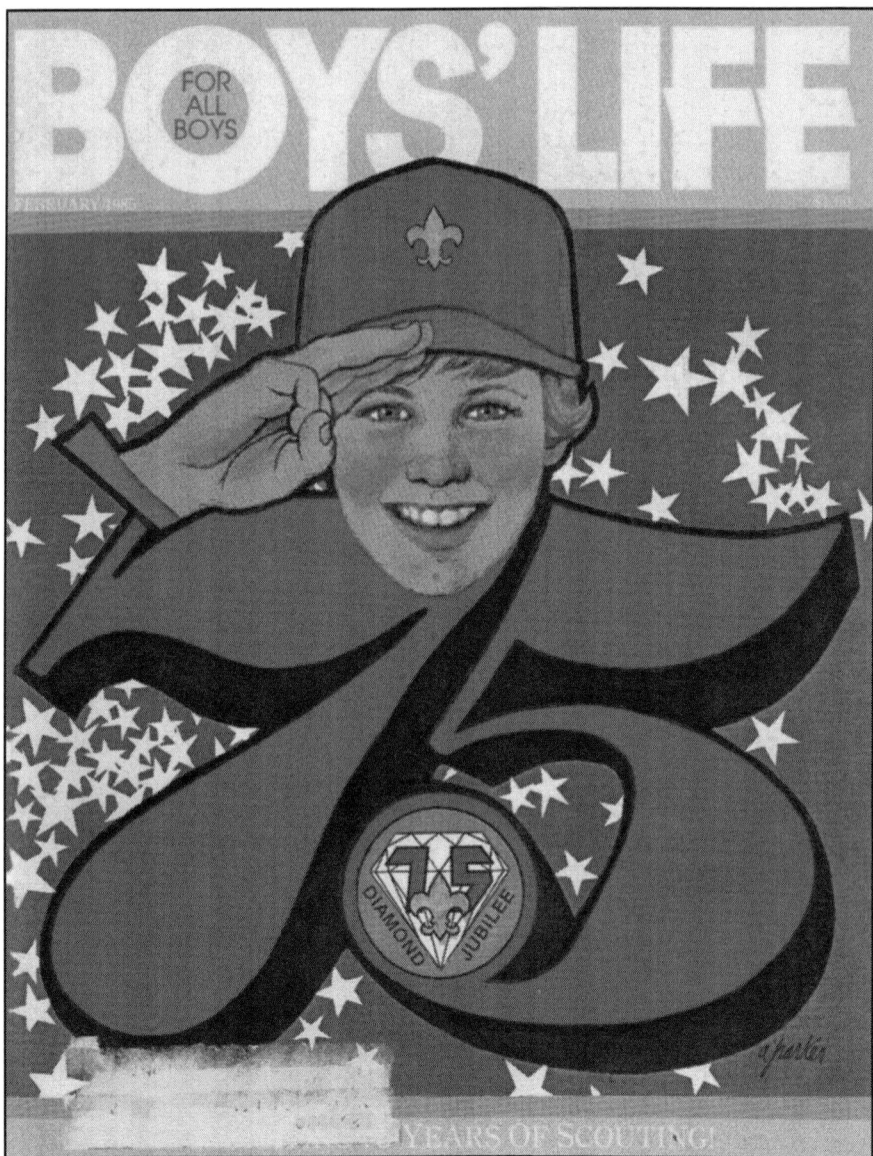

Boys' Life Magazine Cover, February 1985. Boys' Life magazine is an official publication of the Boy Scouts of America. George Barton of Somerville, MA, published the first edition in January 1911. He listed the publisher's address as "7 Water Street, Boston, Mass." It was called Boys' and Boy Scouts' Magazine - a reference to the three competing scouting groups in the US at that time. The first two issues consisted of 8 pages and were not widely distributed. The March 1911 issue went to 48 pages with a two-color cover and is generally considered the first issue of the magazine. In June 1912, Boy Scouts of America purchased the magazine for $6000 - a price figured by paying $1 per subscriber. (Courtesy: Boys' Life magazine, Boy Scouts of America)

1990
Coming Together

The last decade of the 20th century saw BSA looking outside the United States. Delegations from the BSA traveled to Russia and to the Vatican. At home, BSA recognized the growth of the Hispanic population in the United States by creating programs not only aimed at recruitment but also at spreading understanding. The number of Scouts had fallen, so Scouting tried some unconventional approaches including in-school and urban outreach programs. National Jamborees were held in 1993 and 1997 at Fort A.P. Hill in Virginia.

Locally, there were several milestone events during the 1990's in Boston Minuteman Council. The Greater Boston Council and the Minuteman Council joined to form the Boston Minuteman Council in 1994. A new group, the Knights of Storer was formed to help improve T.L. Storer Scout Reservation in 1997. MassJam was held in 1994 and 1999, bringing Scouts from all over New England to North Falmouth for a weekend of fun and competitions.

U.S.S. Constitution. Boston, 1997.
Scouts visit the U.S.S. Constitution in Charlestown, MA. On July 22, 1997, the U.S.S. Constitution celebrated its 200th anniversary by sailing under her own power for the first time in 116 years. Trips to the U.S.S. Constitution remain popular with Cubs and Scouts.

Cub Scouts, Pinewood Derby, 1999. Cub Scouts build and race wooden cars in this much-anticipated annual event. Cars are raced side-by-side down a track. The winner on this three-car track would go on to race other winners. The first Pinewood Derby was held in 1953 in California. It was created by Don Murphy, Cub Master of Cub Scout Pack 280C. He started the event because his own son was too young to race in the Soapbox Derby. The first article about the Pinewood Derby appeared in <u>Boys' Life</u> magazine in 1954. The first official Pinewood Derby kit was available through Boy Scouts in 1955.

Pinewood Derby Winners, circa 1995.

Cub Scout Crafts, 1996. As early as 1916, Wolf Cub Scouting was started by Baden-Powell in England and quickly spread to Europe. Baden-Powell based the original concept on Rudyard Kipling's Jungle Book.

By the 1920's, US boys and parents were trying to bring a cub scouting program to the United States. After years of study and meetings, a demonstration program - Cubbing - was finally begun in the US in 1930 with about 5000 boys enrolled in test Councils. It proved immensely popular, and by 1933, Cubbing was formally opened nation-wide. (The name Cub Scouts was not adopted until 1945.) Originally, Cubs were ages 9 - 12. In 1949, the entry age was lowered to age 8. Tiger Cubs were added in 1982.

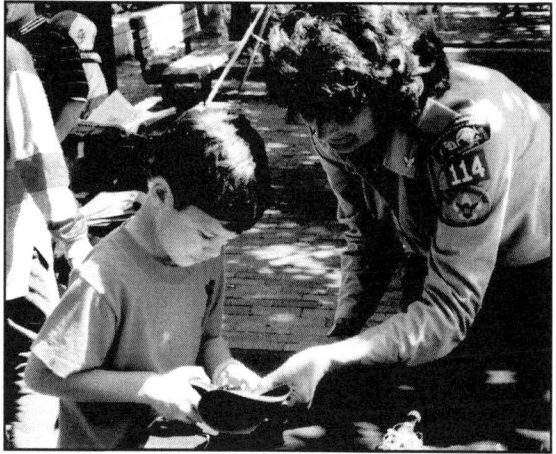

When Cubbing first began, Packs were led by Boy Scout den chiefs, with mothers playing an "advisory" role. Den mother registration increased over the first few years of the program, with approximately 1100 Den mothers registered in Scouting by 1938. Registration for Den mothers became mandatory in 1948. Since its inception, Cub Scouts has grown to almost 1.7 million members (2005), making it the largest division of Boy Scouts of America.

Pack 5, West Roxbury, circa 1995. Saint Theresa's Church.

(Top) Archery, archery range at unidentified camp, Circa 1990. (Bottom) Webelos Woods archery, 1998. Archery was one of the original merit badges awarded to Boy Scouts. About 1.3 million Scouts have earned the Archery Merit Badge. Cub Scouts can earn the Archery Pin and Archery Belt Loop for successfully completing the requirements. Boy Scouts has always had a strong Native American identification in its programs. This is probably due to Ernest Thompson Seton's program called Woodcraft Indians. Baden-Powell had studied Seton's program and was impressed. Seton and Baden-Powell met in 1906 and exchanged ideas about Scouting.

Canoeing, probably Parker Mountain Scout Reservation, Circa 1995. The Canoeing Merit Badge was introduced in 1927. It is the ninth most popular merit badge earned by Scouts, with 2.7 million Scouts earning the badge since its introduction. First Aid is the most popular merit badge.

T.L. Storer Scout Reservation, Rifle Range, 1995. Scouts can earn merit badges in Rifle Shooting and Shotgun Shooting, (both introduced in 1988). The original merit badge for shooting - Marskmanship - was introduced in 1911. In 1966, Marksmanship was replaced by Rifle and Shotgun Shooting. That merit badge was divided into separate rifle and shotgun merit badges in 1988.

MassJam, Swing, 1994. This swing was created by Scouts to demonstrate lashing skills. MassJam is held every four years and attracts Scouts from all over New England. This event is held at the Barnstable County Fairgrounds in North Falmouth, MA. (Courtesy: Collection Bob and Maryjane Wanamaker)

T.L. Storer Scout Reservation, Dining Hall, 1996. The dining hall seats about 400 Scouts, giving everyone plenty of room to spread out on the rustic pine tables and benches. The rafters display signs and banners left by Scout troops over the last 50 years. Check out the photo of the dining hall from 1975 on page 66.

Camp Sayre, Trading Post, circa 1995. The Trading Post is always a popular stop with campers.

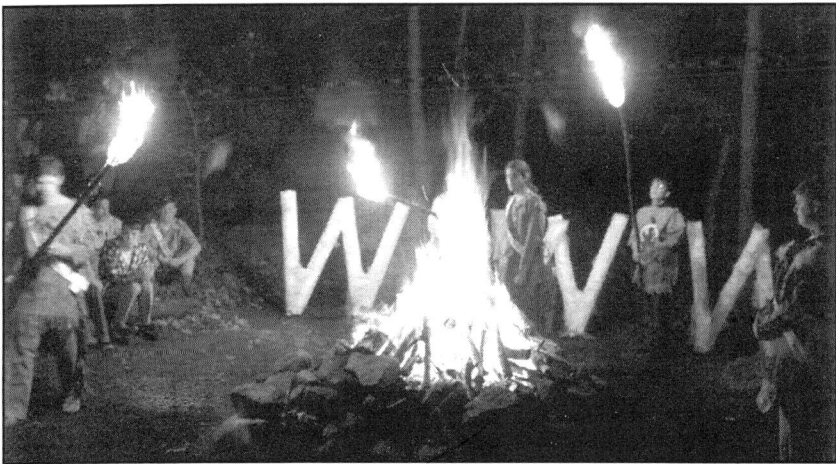

Order of the Arrow Campfire, circa 1995. Order of the Arrow (OA) is an honor society within Boy Scouts. Created in 1915 in Pennsylvania to recognize Scouts who were deemed by their peers as exemplary, it was originally called Wimachtendienk, a Lenape Indian word for brotherhood. The first rituals for OA were written by a 32nd degree Mason, and blend Masonic structure with Native American lore and rituals. By 1921, the society was renamed as Order of the Arrow and had spread to other camps in the northeast. Through the 1920's and 1930's, OA continued to grow as an experimental program. It was formally recognized by Boy Scouts in 1948. The WWW at the campfire is part of the lore of the OA.

"Good Scout" award, East Boston, 1995. Mayor Tom Menino presents "Good Scout" award to Benito and Debora Tauru of East Boston, July 12, 1995.

Probably Concord Boy Scouts, 1998. These Scouts are all equipped with gardening tools - shovels, clippers, and such. While we don't know if this was a Scout's Eagle project, community service is a big part of Boy Scouts. Annually Scouts donate hundreds of thousands of hours to our communities. Some of this is in pursuit of an Eagle rank; some hours are organized around Troop activities. In 1997, the Boy Scouts committed to providing 200 million service hours for the United States. The BSA created the "Service to America" award which could be earned through 12 hours of service. In 2004, a new program was started called "Good Turn for America. Scouts can earn the patch and then smaller "rockers" for each year that Scouts complete the service requirement. Scouts can earn rockers for each year from 2004-2009.

2000

Making a Difference

The first decade of the 21st century was an exciting time in Boston Minuteman Council. About 50 Scouts traveled internationally to the World Jamboree and the Canadian National Jamborees in 2007. In May 2009, the Scouting world came to Boston when we hosted an international event for the King of Sweden.

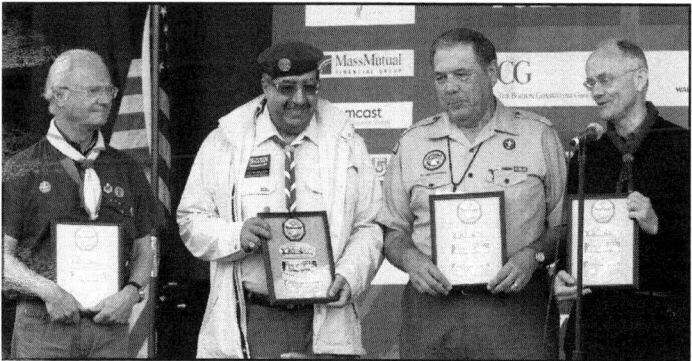

Richard Egan

After years of planning, fund-raising, and building, the new Council headquarters opened at Camp Sayre in Milton, MA in 2006. Named for principal benefactor Richard Egan, The Egan Center has offices, conference rooms, a training center, a Scout shop, and an indoor pool. Egan, who died in 2009, was co-founder of EMC and former Ambassador to Ireland. He was a generous friend to Scouting.

King of Sweden Breakfast, Boston, 2009. In May 2009, Boston Minuteman Council hosted an international gathering of Scout executives. His Majesty, King Carl XVI Gustaf of Sweden (far left), honorary chair of World Scouting, was in Boston to accept a $3M donation to World Scouting Gifts for Peace Program. His Highness, Prince Faisal (second from left) presented the check on behalf of King Abdullah of Saudi Arabia. Robert Mazzuca, Chief Scout Executive Boy Scouts of America (second from right) and Lars Kolind, Chairman of World Scout Foundation (right) were at that event. More photos page 91.
(Courtesy: John Munson, Beacon Photography)

Klondike Derby, Breakfast Challenge, circa 2003. Klondike Derbies began in 1949 to celebrate the pioneering spirit of the Klondike Gold Rush. Typically, Scouts travel from station to station, trying to pass challenges (a breakfast-cooking challenge is shown above) and gain points. The highlight of the day is a dog sled race where Scouts build and pull a sled. Some winters, this proves challenging as there is not always reliable snow cover.

Tiger Cub, Pinewood Derby, 2003. Tiger Cub Scouts began in 1982 in response to younger boys who wanted to get involved in Scouting. Boys who are age 7 or who have completed kindergarten can become Tiger Cubs.

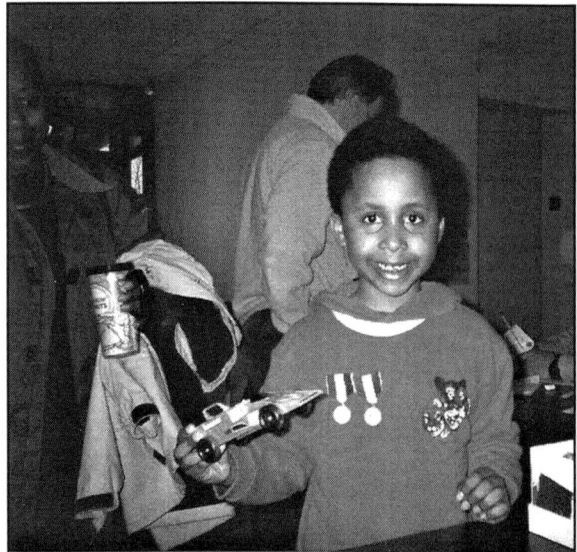

T.L. Storer Scout Reservation, Waterfront, circa 2005 (top and bottom). The waterfront at T.L. Storer is always one of the most popular places at camp. Note the paddle boats in the bottom photo. Since opening its doors to Scouts in 1950, T.L. Storer has been providing summer memories for generations of Scouts. Many of these alumni now belong to the Knights of Storer (KOS), a volunteer group which formed in 1997. KOS raises money and donates services for repair and building of camp facilities. They host work parties which greatly improve the camp every year. Their annual August reunion draws staff, camp alumni, and others to reminisce and share history of the camp. Their motto: "We will give back to camp more than camp gave to us."

COPE, T.L. Storer Scout Reservation, 2000. Challenging Outdoor Personal Experience (COPE) is a program which uses outdoor challenges to build confidence and teamwork. Using high- and low-ropes courses, repelling, and obstacles, Scouts learn to work together to achieve goals. Scouts challenge themselves physically and mentally. Scouts must be 13 years old to participate in the COPE program. Shown here, Scouts on climbing wall.

T.L. Storer Scout Reservation, Archery Range, circa 2005. Since its beginnings, archery has been part of the Scout program. Native American lore, rituals, and skills were woven into the original Scouting program - and remain important. One major change began in the 1970's was to introduce more accurate and culturally sensitive Native American lore and history into the Scouting program including respect for Native American spiritual symbols and rites.

Council Camporee, Thompson Island, Boston, 2002. 1400 Scouts from all over the Council camped for a weekend on Thompson Island, one of the Boston Harbor Islands. While on the island, Scouts could explore the 240 acre island with its views of Boston (seen in the background in this photo). The camporee was held October 19 and 20.

Council Camporee, Thompson Island, Boston, 2002. Scouts from Troop 10 East Boston and a troop from Stoneham set up camp on Thompson Island. Bridge in background is Long Island Bridge connecting Quincy with Moon Island and Long Island.

Webelos, probably Webeolos Woods, 2002. Webelos began in 1941 to provide a better transition from Cub Scouting to Boy Scouting. Originally, it was a rank earned during their last few months of Cub Scouts. Over time, Webelos has expanded to a 2-year program. Webelos originally was an acronym for the ranks of Cub Scouts: Wolf, Bear, Lion, Scout. Lion rank was dropped in 1967 favor of expanding the Webelos program to a full year. Webelos instead came to stand for "We'll Be Loyal Scouts."

Century of Values, Mural, 2009. Michigan Scouters commissioned a mural depicting highlights of the last century of Scouting. They traveled all over the US in 2008-9 presenting prints to local councils. (Left) Howie Nelles, Harold Pinkham (Development Director), Matt Thornton (Scout Executive), Ray Theberge (Council Commissioner), and a Michigan Scouter. The print is now on display at the Egan Center.

Webelos Pack 149, Concord, King of Sweden Breakfast, 2009.
These Webelos were among the 250 Scouts from all over the Council
who were selected to attend the breakfast. (Courtesy: John Munson,
Beacon Photography)

King of Sweden Breakfast, 2009. King Carl XVI Gustaf is honorary
chair of World Scouting. While he was in Boston to accept King
Abdullah's gift, His Majesty presented awards to 14 Boston Scouts
for exceptional achievements. (Left) His Majesty and Eagle Scout
Michael Browne. Browne's project, Get the Lead Out of Fishing, has
won numerous awards including the President's Environmental Youth
Award, a Medal of Merit and a Hornaday Badge from Boy Scouts,
and represented the United States at a United Nations environmental
program in Sweden. (Courtesy: Bruce Showstack)

Troop 546, Stoneham, circa 2005. Scouts learn about ropes.

Pack 377, Belmont, circa 2005. Cub Scouts from Pack 377 in Belmont get ready to march in parade.

Camp Memories

When many people think of Boy Scouts, they think of camping. Many Scouts' fondest memories are being out in the woods with their troop or den. Since the earliest days of Scouting, Boston Minuteman Council has been fortunate to have many generous supporters who have donated land and funds for camps. Early newspaper stories routinely reported on new camps and Scout opportunities.

While many of our camps continue to thrive (T.L. Storer, Camp Massasoit) and make camp memories, other camps have passed out of Council hands.

Take a "visit" to our camps and remember what it was like when young Scouts first plunged into the cold, clear water of a camp pond. Sing along with favorite camp songs around the campfire. Remember what it was like to line up for chow at the dining hall.

Loon Pond Camp Patch, 1938.

We have assembled camp memorabilia including patches, programs, songs, and photos to help you bring back your own camp memories.

T.L. Storer Scout Reservation Pennant. Circa 1970.

Early Camps

As Scout Troops formed and excitement about Scouting spread, Troops and Councils established their own camps. Sometimes land was loaned for temporary camps that lasted only a season or two. Other camps consisted of thousands of donated acres for permanent camps. Some of the camps are only remembered now as a mention in a newspaper or a handwritten note on the bottom of an old photo. We can read a passing reference to "Camp Jackson" or see a photo of "Camp Cobbett" - but have no other information about them. Other camps have decades of history and active alumni organizations.

Camp Brochures, Camp Manning (1930), Loon Pond Camp (Circa 1955). These were distributed to Scoutmasters to advertise the camps. In 1955, Loon Pond Camp cost $16 per Scout per week.

ELEVENTH SEASON

JUNE 29 1930

CAMP MANNING

"As good as the Best"

AUGUST 24 1930

POMP'S POND

BALLARDVALE   MASSACHUSETTS

UNDER THE AUSPICES OF

THE MALDEN COUNCIL, INC.,
BOY SCOUTS OF AMERICA
50 PLEASANT ST., MALDEN, MASS.
TEL. MALDEN 2865

Every Scout in Camp!

CAMP MANNING, a Camp for Boys, is operated by the Malden Council Inc., Boy Scouts of America, for the purpose of helping parents solve the ever-present and important problem of their boy's summer. It is the aim of the Council to provide for the Scouts and prospective Scouts of its Cities and Towns an opportunity to attend a properly organized, well conducted camp, having a healthful, constructive, well-balanced schedule of out-of-door land and water activities. The camp is not operated for profit and the cost is purposely kept as low as possible in order that even those boys in more humble circumstances may have the benefit of such a program.

This is the Eleventh Season and during this entire time there has been no fatality, no serious accident, and a practical absence of other than minor illnesses.

ADVENTURE – *That's Scouting!*
CAMPING – *That's Adventure!*

LOON POND CAMP

PREPARE FOR CAMP NOW!

Camp Jackson, Framingham, 1921.

Camp Merrymount, 1921. This camp was operated by the Quincy Council in Pembroke, MA on Oldham Pond. This shot shows the mess tent. In 1919, it cost $6 per week to attend camp.

Camp Manning, Ribbons, Circa 1925. Scouts would have sewn these on their camp uniforms to let others know how many years they had attended Camp Manning.

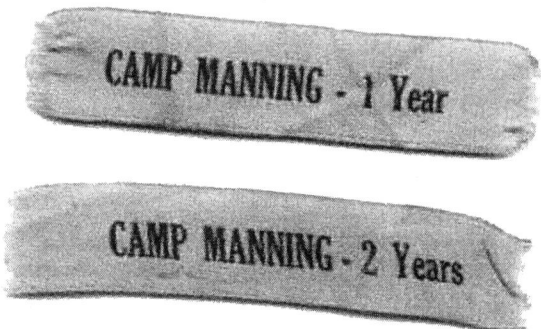

CAMP MANNING - 1 Year

CAMP MANNING - 2 Years

Loon Pond Camp, Pennant, 1925.

BSA

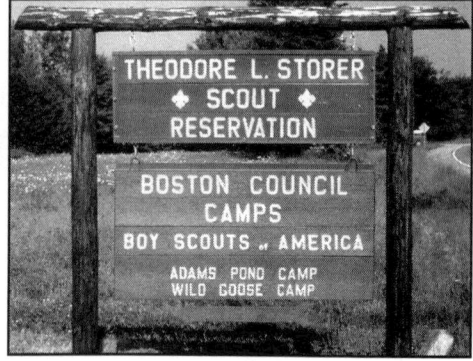

T. L. Storer Scout Reservation, Adams Pond Camp. Wild Goose Camp, Parker Mountain Scout Reservation, Camp Signs, Circa 1970's-1980's.

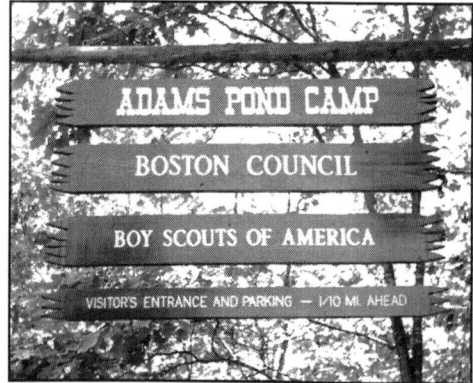

Camp Ted, Badge, 1939. Camp Ted (named for Theodore Storer, who donated the land) was operated by the Cambridge Council The 13-acre site was located on Lexington Street in Waltham, adjacent to the Cabot YMCA reservation. The camp was designed to provide weekend camping opportunities located "3 miles from the end of the Waverly car line." Scout Troops could submit plans and applications to build their own cabins.

Camp Oak, Bedford, Camp Sign, Circa 1960.

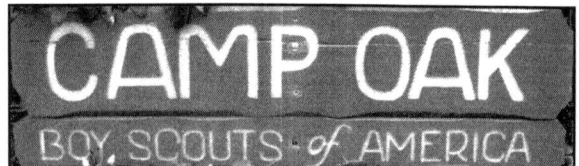

Camp Sachem, Patch, Circa 1950. Patches were worn on camp shirts. The 3 on the patch indicates that this was the third year for this camper.

Camp Massasoit, Leather Neckerchief Slide, 1951.

Mile Swim Patch, Circa 1950. This was awarded after completing a measured mile swim. Worn on swim trunks.

Camp Quinapoxet, Patch, 1975. This 50th Anniversary Patch lists all the dates and locations of the camp: Jefferson, MA 1925; Charlton, MA 1926-1927; Rindge, NH 1928-1975.

Camp Fellsland, Pennant, Circa 1935. Felt pennants were popular bedroom decorations through the 1960's. Many camps had souvenir pennants available for Scouts to take home.

Camp Songs

Every camper has favorite songs sung around the campfire. A few more creative Scouts and Scouters create songs specifically for their favorite camps. Here are a few we have found from years past...

Adams Pond Song

(Tune: "We Will Rock You" by Queen)

Buddy we're not boys, making big noise,
Here at Adams Pond, gonna be a big man some day.

We got dirt on our face, no big disgrace,
It's from working hard all over the place!

Singing! We are, we are Adams! We are, we are Adams!

Buddy, we are young men, good men,
See it in our eyes, gonna take on the world today!

Hear us singing our song, doesn't take long,
No is gonna tell us that we are wrong!

Singing! We are, we are, Adams! We are, we are, Adams!

Buddy we are camp men, proud men,
Spirit is our thing! Gonna tell all the world today.

We've got a smile on our face, no time to waste,
You should know by now that Adams is the place!

Singing! We are, we are Adams! We are, we are Adams!

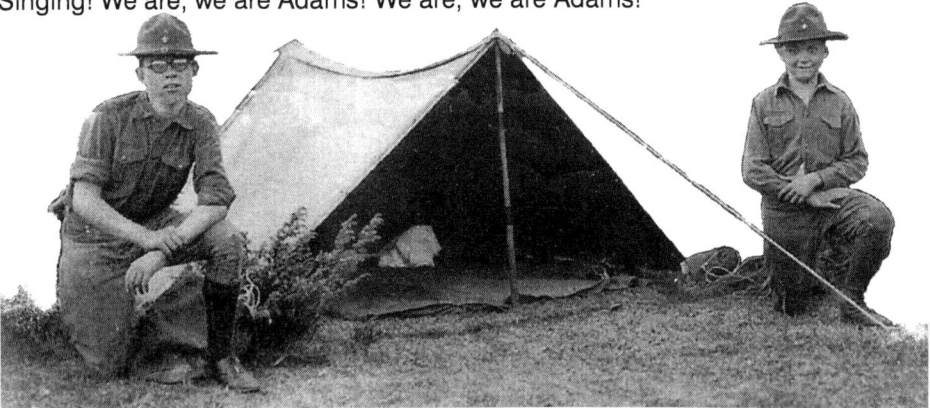

Troop 7, West Newton, 1923.

Parker Mountain Camper
(Tune: "The Yankee Doodle Boy" by George M. Cohan)

I'm a Parker Mountain camper, Parker Mountain all the way.
A real-live statue of the ideal Scout, working and playing all day.

I've got that Parker Mountain spirit, Parker Mountain all the way.
Oh, Parker Mountain here I come, marching o'er the hilltops.

I am a Parker Mountain boy!

Wild Goose Camp Staff Song
(Tune: "As the Caissons Go Rolling Along,"
Army Artillery Song by Gen. Edmund L. Gruber)

We're the men from the hill, we can do it and we will!
As the Goose Men go rolling along.
We are brave, we are strong, hear us sing our mighty song!
As the Goose Men go rolling along.

For it's Wild Goose...'Cause the Goose Men are loose!
Hear us sing our mighty song! (Wild Goose!)

For wherever we go, you will always know,
That the Goose men go rolling along! (Keep 'em rolling)
As the Goose Men go rolling along! (Hi-o!)

Camp Sachem
(Tune: "Jingle Bells" by James Lord Pierpont)

Camp Sachem, Camp Sachem, located far away.
Oh, what fun it is to go and get stuck up in the clay, oh!

Camp Sachem, Camp Sachem, located far away.
Oh, what fun it is to carve a neckerchief slide all day.

Dashing to the dining hall, and the canteen, too.
Then you go swimming, and we will rescue you.
Get Merit Badges every day, Do a Good Turn daily, too.
And you will find that you can say, the Staff men are for you.

Oh, Camp Sachem, Camp Sachem, located far away.
Here's your chance to learn things quick, so sign up right away!

Camp Manning, Camp Handbook, Circa 1930. The Scout Vesper is usually sung around the campfire at the end of the evening. This song is set to the traditional Christmas tune of "O, Tannenbaum" also known as "Maryland, My Maryland."

T.L. Storer Scout Reservation, Campfire, 2007. At the end of every camper's day, there is the special time spent around the campfire. Scouts perform traditional skits that everyone has seen a million times before - and campers still laugh at all the funny parts. Songs with silly lyrics are sung over and over ("This is the song that never ends...it just goes on and on my friends") till no one can sing another note. Spooky stories about ax murderers loose in the woods have sent more than one camper reaching for his flashlight at sounds outside the tent after lights out.

The campfire is about sharing. Campers take turns telling each other stories. Bonds are formed that can last a lifetime. This is what Scout camps are all about.

And at its heart, those friendships are what Scouting is all about.

(Courtesy: Private collection)

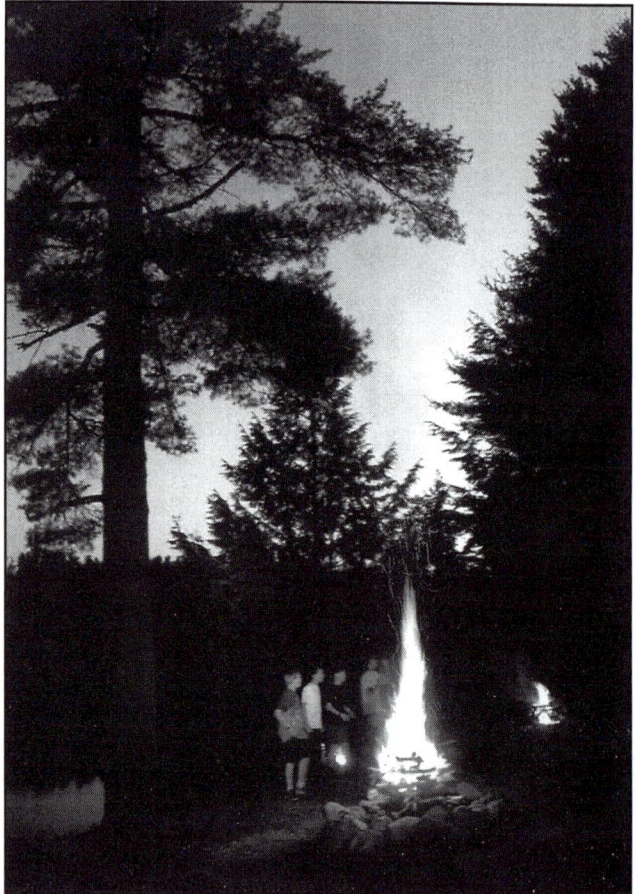